READ. IN A DIFFERENT Light

READ IN A DIFFERENT Light

Stories of Loners, Outcasts, and Rebels

From the Editors of READ Magazine

The Millbrook Press
Brookfield, Connecticut

Library of Congress Cataloging-in-Publication Data
Read in a different light : stories of loners, outcasts, and rebels /
from the editors of Read magazine.
p. cm.
Contents: I now walk into the wild / Ted Hoey — Lov'd alone / Catherine
Gourley — Mountain lion / Jean Stafford — Chameleon / Jordan Phillips
— A man called horse / Dorothy M. Johnson — Country of the blind /
H.G. Wells — Charles / Shirley Jackson — Taming of the shrew / adapted
by Regan Oaks — Punishment / adapted by Charlotte Bronte —
Prometheus / Kate Davis.
ISBN 0-7613-1615-9 (lib. bdg.)
1. Individuality Literary collections. [1. Individuality Literary collections.]
I. Read magazine.
PZ5. R198416 2000
[Fic]—dc21   99-36120 CIP

Published by The Millbrook Press, Inc.
2 Old New Milford Road
Brookfield, Connecticut 06804
www.millbrookpress.com

Read is a literature magazine published for students in middle and senior high school by the Weekly Reader Corporation. Published biweekly during the school year, the magazine features the best of contemporary young adult fiction and nonfiction with classical literature adaptations and historical theme issues. The Best of *Read* series celebrates the magazine's fiftieth anniversary.

Introduction

From childhood's hour I have not been
As others were—I have not seen
As others saw—I could not bring
My passion from a common spring.
From the same source I have not taken
My sorrows' I could not awaken
My heart to joy at the same tone;
And all I lov'd, I lov'd alone.

Edgar Allan Poe, "Alone"

Have you ever felt as if you didn't belong anywhere? Have you ever thought, like Edgar Allan Poe, that all you loved, you loved alone? Or, like Jane Eyre, have you ever resisted the unfair labels others have tried to put on you because of that?

In celebration of fifty years of publishing, the editors of *Read* magazine are proud to bring you this collection of stories about people who live in a different light. For some, being different is a painful challenge. Others revel in it. For still others, however, their unique light is a source of strength and even inspiration to make the world a better place for all.

The stories in this volume in the Best of *Read* series are both fiction and nonfiction. Some come from mythology, others from the imaginations of authors who have also experienced at one time or another being an outcast or a loner. Still others—such as the sad story of Chris McCandless, who trekked into the Alaskan wilderness in hopes of becoming one with nature—come from newspaper headlines. Each story has appeared in the pages of *Read* magazine over the years, and each explores what it is like to "have not been as others were. . . ."

Forget about what everyone else is doing, find a comfortable chair, and read on . . . in a different light.

Contents

PART II
THE OUTCASTS

PART III
The Rebels

READ IN A DIFFERENT Light

PART I
The Loners

"I Now Walk Into the Wild"

by Ted Hoey

CHRIS MCCANDLESS CALLED HIMSELF AN EXTREMIST.
HE SHUNNED MODERN CIVILIZATION AND WALKED INTO
THE WILD TO BECOME ONE WITH NATURE.

*E*arly one April morning in 1992, James Gallien was driving south from Fairbanks to Anchorage when he saw a hitchhiker in the snow beside the road. The young man carried a small pack and a rifle. Nothing unusual, James thought. After all, this was Alaska. James stopped and offered him a ride.

The traveler introduced himself as Alex. "Alex?" James repeated.

"Just Alex."

Despite his refusal to reveal his name or background, Alex proved to be a good companion during the three-hour drive to the edge of Denali National Park. He laughed and chatted and asked sensible questions about the small game in that part of the country and about the kinds of berries and plants that were safe to eat. Clearly,

Alex was looking forward to a wilderness adventure, but James was worried. The region was still buried under winter snowpack. All Alex had for food was ten pounds of rice. He had no compass, only a tattered road map he'd picked up at a gas station. His rifle, a .22-caliber with a telescopic sight, hardly seemed suitable for a land of moose, wolves, and grizzlies.

James tried to talk Alex into giving up his plan or at least going on to Anchorage where he could buy more suitable equipment. "I'll be fine with what I've got," said Alex. "I'm absolutely certain I won't run into anything I can't deal with on my own."

Impressed by the young man's enthusiasm and determination, James agreed to drive him to the town of Healy and an old mining track called the Stampede Trail. Before setting out, Alex gulped down a tuna sandwich offered by James and accepted a pair of the older man's rubber boots. At the same time, Alex insisted on leaving behind the map, his watch, and all the money he had—85 cents. "I don't want to know what time it is," he said cheerfully, "or what day it is or where I am."

"What if something happens to you out there?" James asked. "Do your parents or some friends know what you are about to do?"

The reply was calm and matter-of-fact, but shocking nevertheless. "Nobody knows of my plans. And I haven't spoken to my family in nearly three years."

Alex stepped out of the truck, pulled a camera from his pack, and asked James to take a photograph of him as he started his adventure. Then with a glowing smile, he set off along the snow-covered trail. It was Tuesday, April 13, 1992.

Who was this mysterious young man and what drove him into the wilderness of Alaska, alone?

His name was Christopher "Alex" McCandless, and he could have lived in luxury. He grew up in Annandale, Virginia, outside Washington, D.C. His father and mother ran an aerospace consulting firm, and business was good. His childhood had all the positive parts of the American dream—a younger sister, Carine, with whom he was very close, plus six half siblings from his father's first marriage. Chris grew up happy in a loving family.

But there was always something unusual about Chris, something that made him avoid the expected. As early as third grade, a teacher told Chris's parents that their son "marched to a different drummer." As he grew older, Chris showed more signs of having a restless soul. In high school, he was an excellent student and captain of the cross-country team. But he also formed a group he named the Road Warriors and led its members on "suicide runs" through swamps and up wooded hills, trying to get lost. On mountain hiking trips with his father, he would always seek out the most challenging, most dangerous trails.

He was fearless, his father said. Chris just didn't think the odds applied to him. More than once, his family tried to pull him back from the precipice. And yet there was also another side to the daring, risk-taking Chris. He worried about the homeless. He couldn't understand how so many people could ignore the poor and downtrodden.

Often he went into the nation's capital to talk to homeless people and buy them meals. *Why is life like this?* he asked himself. *Why do humans keep treating each other so badly?*

At Emory University in Atlanta, Chris chose a small room furnished only with a table, a chair, his computer, and a mattress on the floor. He had no telephone. He studied seriously and again proved himself to be an outstanding student. Even so, he turned down all academic honors presented to him. Such awards, he said, were not important. Upon graduation, his parents gave him $20,000 for graduate studies, but Chris donated the entire fund to a famine-relief organization. Then he left town.

In his battered Datsun car, he drove west. When the car broke down in the Arizona desert, Chris buried his valuables and burned what was left of his money—$160. In 120-degree heat, he set off on foot toward the Pacific Coast. Along the way he camped with hoboes, hopped trains, and hitched rides. Gradually, he worked his way northward. Those he met along the way remembered him as charming and funny even if he was a dreamy, eccentric loner.

Chris kept a journal and at times wrote short letters to friends he had made in his travels. One was Wayne Westerberg, the owner of a grain elevator in South Dakota who had given Chris a job. Chris stayed only a short time and seemed distressed whenever Wayne presented him with the paycheck Chris had earned. After quitting the job and moving on, Chris wrote to Wayne: "My days are more exciting when I am penniless and have to forage around for my next meal. I've decided I am going to live this life for some time to come. The freedom and simple beauty of it are just too good to pass up."

Although Wayne Westerberg had received a few letters from Chris, the McCandless family had heard nothing of their son. Desperate for news, Chris's parents hired a private investigator to search for their missing son. The search failed.

However, Wayne Westerberg—not knowing that Chris's family was sick with worry—had received still one more message from the mysterious loner. The postcard read: *Greetings from Fairbanks. This is the last you shall hear from me. It was very difficult to catch rides in the Yukon Territory. But I finally got here. . . . It might be a very long time before I return south. If this adventure proves fatal and you don't ever hear from me again, I want you to know you're a great man. I now walk into the wild. Alex.*

And so, the day after mailing the postcard, Chris hitched a ride with James Gallien who, a few hours later, snapped his photograph and watched Chris trek away into the wilderness.

In his journal, Chris recorded what happened next. The walk into the park was rough. A foot of snow covered the ground. Although it was April and spring, temperatures at night still dropped well below freezing. Game was scarce. While crossing a stream, Chris broke through the ice. After covering 28 miles, he came across an old Fairbanks City bus that hunters and trappers had moved into the wild as a shelter. He decided to use the bus as his base camp. Having made it this far and settled in, Chris felt a rush of joy. On a sheet of old plywood on the bus he scrawled a triumphant declaration of independence.

He wrote: *Two years he walks the earth. No phone, no pool, no pets, no cigarettes. Ultimate freedom. An extremist. A voyager whose home is the road. . . . No longer poisoned by civilization he flees, and walks alone upon the land to become lost in the wild. Alexander Supertramp.*

Judging from his journal, Chris's elation ended quickly in the harsh truths of interior Alaska. Included in entries from the first week are such words as "weakness," "snowed in," and "disaster." On May 5, he shot and ate a spruce grouse but had nothing more until he bagged a squirrel on May 9. In the journal, he had written "4th day of famine."

In mid-May, things improved when the snow melted enough to expose edible plants. Chris also became much better at hunting and added duck, goose, and porcupine to his diet. On May 22, he lost a crown from a tooth but took that loss in stride. The next day, he climbed a 3,000-foot butte and saw the whole glorious sweep of Denali Park and the Alaska Range. "CLIMB MOUNTAIN" he wrote in exultant capital letters.

Chris had accepted the idea of hunting animals for survival, and on June 9, he managed to bring down a moose with his .22-caliber. Immediately conscience-stricken, he labored for six days to preserve the meat, feeling it wrong to waste any part of an animal killed for food. He cut up the carcass under a thick cloud of flies and mosquitoes, boiled the internal organs into a stew, and tried to smoke the huge quantity of meat. His effort failed. A journal entry for June 14 reads "Maggots already! Smoking appears ineffective. I now wish I had never shot the moose. One of the greatest tragedies of my life."

Despite everything, life in the wilderness seemed to be changing Chris. Soon after losing the moose meat he wrote "Henceforth will learn to accept my errors, however great they may be." Apparently he was coming to peace with himself. And that was, in part, his reason for walking into the wild. It was more than an adventure. He was on a spiritual quest to become one with nature.

Perhaps he felt he had succeeded. Or perhaps he felt he had failed. Whatever the reason, in early July, his thoughts escaped the wilderness and returned to his family back east. Clearly, his journal entries suggest he was considering returning to civilization after all. On July 3, he wrote: "Family happiness." On a strip of birch bark, he wrote a list of things to do—patch jeans, shave, organize, pack. On July 5, he left the bus and headed back along the Stampede Trail toward the highway. The weather was warm. The food was meager, but enough. His spirits seemed high.

Then came a serious setback. The stream that had been frozen in April and across which he had walked was now running chest-deep, icy cold, and swift. The far bank was 40 yards away—so near and yet so far. Chris weighed his options. The current could carry him away, suck him under, drown him. Even if he managed to fight the current, the freezing temperature of the water would soon zap his energy. Either way, attempting to cross the river was deadly. He turned back for the bus. His journal entry captured his desperation. "Rained in. River looks impossible. Lonely. Scared."

For the rest of July, Chris ate small game, frogs, wild potatoes, wild rhubarb, berries, and mushrooms. He continued to lose weight, but he was surviving. In another week or so, the rains would stop and the river might slow and recede. Before that happened, however, there came a second blow.

The wild sweet pea that grows with and resembles the wild potato was poisonous. Unknowingly, Chris ate the plant and became violently ill. In his journal for August 5 he wrote: "Day 100. MADE IT!" Then he added, "But in weakest condition of life. Too weak to walk out."

He was also too weak to hunt. Over the next ten days, he bagged only five squirrels and a spruce goose. He was slipping toward starvation.

From August 13 to 18, he put nothing more in the pages of his journal than the days of the week. At some point, he tore a blank page from one of his books and wrote a brief farewell message: "I have had a happy life and thank the Lord. Good-bye and God bless all."

Then he crawled into his sleeping bag, one his mother had made for him long ago, and he waited for death to come.

On September 6, moose hunter Butch Killian decided to spend the night at the abandoned bus used as a shelter by local hunters. As he stepped into the bus, a sickening smell hit him. At first he thought a trapper had left some rotting food. Then he saw a sleeping bag and something in it.

Killian did not investigate any further. Wisely, he called the police on his CB radio and told them of his discovery. The next day, Alaska state troopers flew in by helicopter and found Chris's body in the sleeping bag. They also found a note he had written, apparently many weeks before.

S.O.S. I need your help. I am injured, near death, and too weak to hike out of here. I am all alone; this is no joke. Please remain to save me. I am out collecting berries close by and shall return this evening. Thank you, Chris McCandless. August?

Ironies surround the story of Chris McCandless. When the rushing river turned him back, he did not know that salvation was just a quarter-mile downstream. There, the stream entered a narrow canyon spanned by a hand-operated tram. Chris could have climbed into a basket suspended from a steel cable and used pulleys to crank himself across the current rushing below. But then, this was an ingenious construction of civilization, and civilization was what Chris had come to Alaska to escape.

Nor did Chris know that six miles south of the bus, an easy day's walk, was a cabin set up by the National Park Service to provide food and shelter to back-country park rangers. If Chris had not scorned civilization, he would have carried with him into the wilderness the type of map that hikers and hunters use. On this map, he would have noted the shelter's location—and the location of the tram across the gorge, too.

There was one other way Chris might have saved himself. He could have started a forest fire as a distress signal.

But someone who felt that killing a moose was the greatest tragedy of his life would never have sacrificed trees and brush to call attention to his distress.

What was it about modern civilization that Chris so distrusted? What drove him to cut himself off so completely from his family and his friends? Those who knew and loved Chris have no answer.

Perhaps the photograph he took of himself in his final days provides a clue. In this picture, he stands near the bus, under a clear Alaska sky. In one hand, he is holding up the farewell note he had written. His other hand is raised in farewell. He is thin, wasted, but he is smiling. He knew he was dying. His eyes seem to glow with a calm tranquillity—as though he has found the answers to all his questions. He seems to be saying, "I have been one with nature, and I have found my peace."

Lov'd Alone

by Catherine Gourley
a story of the life of Edgar Allan Poe

HIS FOSTER FATHER VOWED TO GIVE THE ORPHANED BOY AN EXCELLENT EDUCATION, BUT HE REFUSED TO GIVE HIM WHAT THE CHILD NEEDED MOST—A FATHER'S LOVE.

A dismal November rain fell over the city of Richmond, Virginia. The driver reined his horse to a stop in front of a boardinghouse on lower Main Street, a temporary home for actors traveling through the city. Hastily, Mr. and Mrs. Usher stepped out of the carriage and hurried to the door. Mrs. Usher carried a dish of cold, greasy chicken legs, covered with a damp towel. "Do you think she'll be much improved today?" she asked her husband.

"My dear, Eliza is never going to get well again."

"What will become of the children?"

Mr. Usher gazed up the stairwell, dimly lit by wall sconces. On the top stair gazing down through the spindles was a three-year-old boy. Mr. Usher smiled. "Hello,

Eddie! We've come to see you." As the couple started up the stairs, Mr. Usher whispered to his wife, "Surely some good family will take the children."

"Eliza told me she has relatives in Baltimore. Perhaps—" She stopped. From the open bedroom door she could hear Eliza's racking cough. "Oh, poor, beautiful Eliza!" Mrs. Usher sobbed.

Mr. Usher picked up Edgar in his arms. "All this rain has kept you from playing outside, hasn't it, lad? Well, it will soon end."

One evening, end it did—the drumming rain *and* the cough.

Edgar stood at the foot of his mother's sickbed and stared at her waxen face and at her black hair streamed across the soiled pillow. "When will Mama wake up?" he asked.

"Not for a long, long time," Mrs. Usher told him. "She wanted you to have this so you should never forget her." She handed him a miniature portrait of Eliza. The boy stared at it and then looked again at the woman in the bed. "Be a good little boy, Eddie, and throw her a kiss and say your good-bye. You must kiss your little sister, Rosalie, too, for she is going away just like you."

"Can't she come with me?"

"No, she is going with Mrs. Mackenzie."

In the hallway, a man and a woman waited. Frances and John Allan were respected people in the community, but they were strangers to the little boy. Mrs. Usher nudged Edgar toward them. Frances knelt and held out her arms, but the man stood stiffly, distressed by the sour odors of sickness that permeated the place. "I have no children, Eddie," the kneeling woman said. "From now on, you shall be my own little boy. Oh, do come here to me!"

Edgar glanced over his shoulder toward the sickroom, but Mrs. Usher had already softly shut the door.

Months later in the Allan home in Richmond, friends gathered for a party. Dressed in a new velvet suit, four-year-old Edgar wandered among the adults. A woman spied the boy and asked her companion, "Is that the child? Such large gray eyes and curly black hair."

"His mother was that beautiful actress who died last autumn of—what was it? Pneumonia?"

"Consumption," the woman said with distaste. "The boy's father was also an actor and…" she leaned forward to gossip, "a drunkard! One day he walked out and was never seen again."

Just then, Frances Allan approached the women. "Good evening, ladies."

"Dear Frances, we were just commenting on what a beautiful child Edgar is," said the woman who had just a moment ago been gossiping about the boy's drunkard father.

Frances beamed. "Eddie can recite rhymes!"

Now John Allan stepped beside her. He, too, was proud of the boy. "He sings and dances like his mother. Here. Off with your shoes, lad." John pulled the child toward him.

Frances told the others, "My John just loves to show Edgar off."

The foster father undid the shiny buckles of the boy's shoes, then lifted him in his stocking feet onto the dining room table. The room grew silent as the guests turned to watch. Edgar began to sing and to dance in an elfish way. When the dance ended, John poured sweet-smelling wine into a teacup, which Edgar lifted in a toast. This, too, had been rehearsed.

"To your fine health, one and all," the child mimicked the adults. Charmed, the guests applauded. "He is such a precious pet," said one.

"Have you adopted him?" asked the woman who knew the secret of Edgar's real father.

Frances glanced quickly at her husband, now helping Edgar from the table. "Of course, Mr. Allan loves children as much as I do. He has sworn to provide Edgar with an excellent education. Why, anyone can see the boy is as bright as a shiny new penny."

"Then surely," the woman said, "Mr. Allan has given the boy his name."

Frances hesitated. "I have not yet persuaded Mr. Allan to adopt Edgar."

"Perhaps Mr. Allan simply requires more time to grow accustomed to the idea," the woman suggested kindly.

"Yes," Frances said. "A little more time."

So began the second childhood of Edgar Poe. The first was brief and tainted with the pain of his mother's illness. But life in the Allan home was all books and learning, velvet suits and shiny buckles. Frances Allan coddled the dark-eyed boy. John Allan praised him for excelling in his studies of Latin and Greek. As the years passed, Edgar learned to shoot and to box and—somewhat annoying to John— to write love poems to pretty girls. More infuriating was the boy's insistence that his foster father publish a book of his poems. John Allan was not a poor man, but neither was he wealthy. The child perplexed him. He was well-mannered and bright, and yet the child seemed to expect a great deal more than he gave. "I was an orphan myself," John Allan complained to Frances. "Nobody gave me all the things I have handed to Edgar—clothing, a good home, an education. He shows no gratitude." Frances wished to remind her husband of the one thing he had not yet given—the legal name of Allan. But she said nothing.

A few days later, a visitor arrived at the apartment of Master Clark, Edgar's schoolteacher. "Why, Mr. Allan!" the teacher said in surprise. "How can I serve you?"

John Allan set a small bundle of papers on the master's desk. "What is your opinion of these rhymes? Are they any good?"

"Oh, yes, Edgar's verses." The teacher nodded. "They are indeed good. Edgar is a born poet."

"He wishes me to publish this bundle into a book. I vowed to see what I could do—upon your approval that is."

The schoolteacher looked grim. "I will be frank. I like the boy very much, but you have spoiled him. He is an excellent pupil but arrogant and mischievous. In short, sir, to publish a book when he is but 14 would excessively flatter his self-esteem."

John Allan straightened his shoulders. "The women in the house have spoiled him, not I. As for the poems, I shall do as you say and forget them." He turned for the door.

"Forget them? Oh, I should not go that far. Your son is a credit to you, sir. I'm certain that one day, he—"

John Allan interrupted him coldly. "Edgar Poe is my *ward*, not my son. Good day."

Dressed in white muslin, Jane Stanard was feeding pigeons in the garden. In a shaft of golden sunlight birds fluttered above her. The vision stunned Edgar. "Is she your mother?" Edgar said to Rob. "No, she is Helen, a goddess."

"She's my mother," Rob insisted. "Who is Helen?"

Edgar laughed. "The most beautiful woman in all of ancient Greece. She was the reason the Greeks fought the Trojans." Rob stared at him blankly.

Jane greeted the boys who entered the garden. "So *you* are Edgar Poe. Rob talks about you all the time." Edgar stared at her as if in a trance. Her dark eyes were so like the eyes in the miniature portrait of his mother that Edgar had treasured all of his childhood. "Rob tells me you are a poet. When you come to visit again, you must bring some of your poems and read to me."

Edgar returned again and again. He sat with his friend's mother in the garden and read his verses to her, the very same verses his foster father had refused to publish.

In youth's spring it was my lot
To haunt of the wide earth a spot
The which I could not love the less
So lovely was the loneliness.

Jane Stanard wondered how a boy so young could understand loneliness and melancholy. Although 14, he had traveled with his foster father and studied in England. Even so, this boy was a world apart from her own son. "Why do you frown each time you mention Mr. Allan's name?" she asked one afternoon.

"He hates me. He wants me out of the house."

"That can't be true, Edgar."

"He praises, then scolds and accuses me of idleness. What else am I to think?" Edgar did not tell her the awful secret he had just discovered. His foster father had a mistress. Jane saw the brooding in the boy's eyes and placed her hand gently on his cheek.

"Do not linger long in those dark corners of your imagination, Edgar," she warned.

"I am not like others," he told her. "I see things differently. Oh, the things I see in my dreams—shadows and demons!"

"Yes, but you also see beauty. One day you will be a wonderful poet, but you must not let the darkness swallow you."

At a time when his foster father had turned cold to him, Jane's kind words filled Edgar with hope—and something more. Although he could never and would never speak of it to Rob, Edgar had fallen in love with this beautiful woman who was the very age his own mother would have been—had she lived. "One day I shall write about you," he told Jane.

Jane seemed not to hear him. All during their visit, she had sighed and gazed at her hands. Now she stood and gently told him to leave. "I'm not feeling very well today, Edgar."

A few days later, Rob told Edgar he must not come again to his home. Rob's baby sister had died, and his mother's overwhelming grief had made her seriously ill.

"But I must see her! She'll want to see me."

Rob shook his head. "She sees no one. She speaks to no one. All she does is wail."

That night, Edgar began to write a poem that he titled "To Helen." For days, he worked on the meter and the rhyme, but before he could finish, the news of Jane's death shocked him. For the second time in his young life, death had stolen someone he loved. John Allan did not understand the boy's loss, for he did not understand the affection Edgar had shared with the mother of Edgar's best friend.

"Why is the boy always so moody?" he asked his wife.

"Be patient with him, John. That woman who died was his friend."

"A woman twice his age who died of insanity? My patience grows thin, Mrs. Allan—with you and with Edgar."

Alone in the graveyard at dusk, Edgar sobbed over Jane's tombstone. This was not the first visit to the dead Edgar had made. Nor would it be his last.

Several months later, John Allan inherited a great sum of money. He purchased a large home in Richmond. Nearby was the Royster estate. For the first time since Jane Stanard's death, the curtain of depression lifted from Edgar's shoulders. Elmira Royster was 16 and quite pretty.

She too had noticed the handsome and mysterious romantic young man who was her new neighbor. When Edgar visited, she played the piano. He read her stories of lost love. Mr. Royster, however, did not approve. Edgar Poe was the son of actors.

"Is he not Mr. Allan's heir?" Elmira challenged her father. "Besides, I love him."

Edgar and Elmira managed to find ways of being alone. He signaled her from his bedroom window, waving a white handkerchief. In a private, wooded place, Edgar vowed his undying love. "In January, I am going away to the University of Virginia. I will become a man of letters. Promise me that you'll marry me when I return."

"Marry you? But my father—"

Edgar's dark eyes glinted with mischievousness. "We won't tell your father. At least, not yet. Once I have distinguished myself at the university and published my poems, he will not object to our engagement."

The romance of secret, forbidden love thrilled Elmira. She hugged his neck. "Oh, yes, I'll marry you. But our engagement must be our secret. And you must write to me every day, because you write the most wonderful things, Edgar."

In January, John Allan gave Edgar $110 and bade him farewell. Sixty miles away at the university, Edgar discovered that the rental of his room—No. 13 West Range— did not cover wood for the fireplace nor food nor books nor paper. The other students arrived with trunks of clothing. Some even brought personal servants. Within the first week, Edgar's money was gone, and he had no choice but to purchase his books on credit. At once he wrote to his foster father of his predicament.

Dear Sir, Surely you have underestimated the costs of my education. I am in extreme need of funds . . .

In response, John Allan sent a meager forty dollars with one dollar extra for spending money. Room rent alone cost $15 a month.

It was going to be a long, cold winter.

A dozen boys crowded into room No. 13. They had unbuttoned their ruffled shirts and pushed back their sleeves. As one boy dealt cards, Z. Collins Lee passed a bottle of apple wine around the room. "Go on, Edgar, have a drink," he urged.

Drinking was a new but not a pleasant experience for Edgar. The liquor set his heart pounding. Still, he quaffed the warm wine in a single swallow.

"Why is it you never wait for the water but gulp it down?" Lee asked.

"I don't much like the taste." Suddenly the room was very warm. The liquor flushed his face. His heart pounded. The boys gathered their cards and began to gamble.

Edgar excelled at his studies but not at cards. Each night, his debts mounted. One afternoon, charged with a 60-cent fine at the library, Edgar counted out the coins in his pocket: 45 cents. It was all the money he had. The librarian took it.

"You ought not to drink, Eddie," Lee told him one night. He had come to know Edgar better now, and he felt sorry for him. "You can't carry your liquor and you can't play cards. You always lose."

"How else am I to get some money? Pa has abandoned me."

"What of the girl you left behind? Have you heard from her?"

Edgar shrugged, looking away. "I am too busy studying to worry about Elmira just now." It was a lie. He *had* written letters, many letters, but she had not answered. Elmira had forgotten him.

That was not quite the truth, either. In Richmond, Elmira appeared at the door to her father's library one evening. "Edgar Poe promised to write to me. Has no letter come yet?"

"I told you he was unreliable," her father said. Disappointed and confused, Elmira returned to her room. Downstairs in the library, Mr. Royster opened a drawer and removed a bundle of letters. One by one he dropped them on the fire in the hearth.

John Allan was also receiving letters—letters of debt for Edgar A. Poe. Furious, he traveled to the university. The meeting in room No. 13 was as chilled as the room was damp. John Allan paced, his hands behind his back. "Why do you not burn a fire?"

"I've no money for wood, sir," Edgar answered.

"Because you have gambled it all away."

Edgar answered arrogantly. "If you had provided the funds that you knew I required when you sent me here, I would not have been forced to try to win a few coins to feed myself and clean my clothes."

In the hallway, Z. Collins Lee and the others listened to the heated argument behind the closed door.

John Allan held up fistful of debt notices. "Two thousand dollars! Do you suppose that I will pay these?"

"I supposed you would honor your word and provide the education you promised on the day my mother died."

"You forget yourself, sir. I am *not* your father and therefore not legally responsible for these notes." The words stung. What John Allan said next cut deeper. "You will return to Richmond and work for me in the countinghouse and in that way clear your debts."

"Leave the university? But I have placed at the top of my classes." Edgar mustered his pride and stood straight before his foster father. "I intend to be a man of letters."

"You, sir, are an idler, a gambler, and no better than a thief!"

Edgar had no choice but to return to Richmond. When he called for Elmira. Mr. Royster did not invite him inside the door. His daughter, he told him, was in North Carolina with relatives. Edgar asked for her address, but Mr. Royster informed him that Elmira was to be married to a Mr. Shelton.

"But *we* were engaged," Edgar said. "We made a vow to each other."

Mr. Royster eyed him with distaste. "How would you support her? I understand you were dismissed from the university—"

"Not dismissed, no! Is that what Mr. Allan has told you? It's not true."

"—for gambling and for drunken behavior."

Edgar felt a rage building inside him. He had been unjustly treated, abused by the very person who had sworn at his mother's deathbed to protect him. Before Mr. Royster closed the door on Edgar, he added a final insult. "I assure you, Elmira has quite forgotten all about you and whatever vow you made."

Weeks passed. Edgar worked in the countinghouse, as required, but his relationship with his foster father was strained until, at last, Edgar rebelled. One morning, reminded again by John Allan of his worthlessness, Edgar stormed out of the house. He left with nothing, not even a hat or a coat.

For one day and one night, he wandered the streets. On the second day, angry words flowed from his pen in a letter to his supposed protector. *Sir! My determination is to leave you and find some place in this wide world where I will be treated—not as you have treated me. I request that you send me at once my trunk containing my clothes and books. Send also money enough to book passage to the northern cities.* He signed the letter Edgar Poe, purposely omitting the name Allan.

He received no answer. On the third day, still without money and warm clothing, he reconsidered and wrote a second, softer letter. *Dear Sir, Be so good as to send me my trunk with my clothes—I am in the greatest necessity.*

Still, no trunk, no books, and no money arrived. Desperate, Edgar persuaded the captain of a coal barge to allow him to work for his passage north. He fled Richmond in the night, an orphan still. So ended, bitterly and with pangs of hunger, the second childhood of Edgar Poe.

From here, Poe's life story twisted and turned, tumbled down blind alleys, then retraced its steps and struck out in new directions, as if the poet were lost in a labyrinth. In a way, he was. In Boston, he managed to publish his first book of poems. But it was a thin volume that earned not a single cent—a blind alley. He turned another corner, enlisting in the army. With his athletic abilities and his intelligence, he soon rose in the ranks. But an enlisted man can go only so far. Another dead end. Oh, but if he were an officer . . .

Swallowing his pride, Edgar begged his foster father's forgiveness and asked for his help in securing an appointment to West Point. This time, John Allan gave in. Perhaps he believed a military career could stiffen and discipline the wayward orphan. Yet after a few months, the army dishonorably discharged Edgar for failing to attend drills. Edgar left West Point as he had left Richmond, with nothing but his pride and his imagination in his pockets.

He wound his way downriver to New York City, hoping to sell his stories. But bouts of drinking waylaid him. Eventually, he found his way to Baltimore and at last to the woman and the girl who would change his life forever—his aunt Maria Clemm and his cousin Virginia.

Maria welcomed him into her home as a lost lamb. Although money and food were scarce, Edgar Poe was family, and Maria allowed him to live in the garret. In this tiny attic room, among his mother's relatives at last, Edgar wrote freely. He wrote of murders and morgues, of madness and menace. He wrote of people's predisposition to meanness and evil.

Day after day, his affection deepened for Maria—whom he called Muddy—and for 11-year-old Virginia—whom he called Sissy. "Someday Virginia might make you a devoted wife. She's awfully fond of you, Eddie."

"Sissy is just a child."

"She won't always be so young. As her mother, I must think of her future. There is an uncle who would like her to come live with him."

This news upset Edgar. "Don't send her away! I couldn't live if I lost her, too. You and Sissy are all I have in the world."

"Well," said Muddy. "There's time yet to think about it."

Soon after, word reached Baltimore that John Allan was dying. Maria urged Edgar to make his peace with the man who had once given him a home. "He has mocked my dependence on him and my failure to earn a decent living," Edgar muttered bitterly.

Maria's words softened him. "Surely on his deathbed he will find it in his heart to forgive you!"

And so Edgar scraped up enough money for the journey to Richmond. He bounded up the stairs and entered his foster father's bedroom. The man's eyes were sunken, and his skin was sallow. Yet when he saw Edgar, he mustered energy enough to rage, "Get out! Get out!"

"Sir! I beg you. Allow me to make amends before it is too late," Edgar pleaded.

John Allan reached for a cane beside his bedpost and swung it overhead. "Get out, you blackguard!"

Edgar backed away and descended the stair.

A few days later, John Allan died. He willed his estate to his two illegitimate sons, the children of his mistress. The will made no mention of the orphan Edgar Poe.

Eleven years later, on a cold night in 1845, Edgar sat in the parlor of a home in New York City. A fire burned brightly. All eyes turned to the dark-haired man sitting in the corner. "We would be so honored," they said, "if you should read your poem to us."

The years had been both kind and cruel to Edgar. He had married Virginia, as Muddy had hoped. For years, they had been devoted to each other. Yet—cruelly—like so many of the people Edgar had dared to love, Sissy was dying of the very illness that had killed his mother. He had published stories and poems, and admiration for him as an author had grown. Even so, his work earned him little money with which to live comfortably.

"Very well," he told the guests. "But I prefer that the lights be dimmed."

Then he stood. Gone were the velvet coats and shiny shoe buckles of his youth. His clothes now were well-worn and out of style. Gone too was the lean, athletic body. Still, his voice was strong and hypnotic as he recited the verse that had brought him respect at last as a man of letters. He had titled it "The Raven."

Once upon a midnight dreary while I pondered weak and weary, Over many a quaint and curious volume of forgotten lore . . .

The fire's flames cast long, birdlike shadows across the floor. The guests listened breathlessly.

Ah, distinctly I remember it was in the bleak December,
And each separate dying ember wrought its ghost upon the
floor.

As they listened, each guest wondered, Who was
Lenore of whom the poet had written so passionately?
They knew nothing of his mother Eliza, Jane Stanard,
Elmira Royster.

And the raven, never flitting, still is sitting, still is sit-
ting . . .

Late that night, Edgar made his way home to his small
cottage. He stood in the bedroom doorway and saw
Virginia shivering on her straw mattress. Caterina, Edgar's
brown cat, lay across her chest, providing some meager
warmth. The cat saw him first and perked her ears. Edgar
stepped inside the room and asked with as much cheerful-
ness as he could muster, "Are you any better, Sissy?" He
knew she was not.

"Did you read tonight?"

"Yes. Shall I tell you all about it?"

Virginia nodded weakly, then suddenly a shuddering
cough seized her. She turned her head to mask the blood
she spat up. Edgar draped his overcoat across her legs to
warm her—he had nothing else to offer—then sat at her
side. Her hand in his was cold as stone.

Weeks later, Edgar sat alone in the room. He read
aloud the poem he was writing.

It was many and many a year ago
In a kingdom by the sea,
That a maiden there lived whom you may know
By the name of Annabel Lee;

And this maiden she lived with no other thought
Than to love and be loved by me.

Caterina leapt softly onto Poe's shoulder. He lifted his head to look through the window at the sepulcher where Virginia was buried. Inside his head he heard Jane Stanard's warning: *Do not linger long in those dark corners, Edgar.* The poet answered, "Helen, I cannot escape the dark. It haunts me. I am alone. I am lost."

The room was still. Caterina groomed her paw delicately. Edgar picked up his pen once more.

She was a child and I was a child
In this kingdom by the sea
But we loved with a love that was more than love—
I and my Annabel Lee. . . .

For months after Virginia's death, Edgar cared little if he should live or die. He drank himself into stupors. His heart knocked so loudly he wondered that Muddy couldn't hear it. And yet he was able to write. Muddy encouraged him to publish his own magazine. To do that required money. Edgar pulled himself together and tried still again to make his life work. In June 1848, he traveled back to Richmond to give a lecture and, he hoped, to raise much-needed funds for his new magazine. While there, he found a reason to stay. By coincidence, he met again his childhood sweetheart, Elmira Royster.

Her pleasure at seeing him after so many years was obvious. She, too, had lost her spouse. For three months, Edgar lingered in Richmond, much longer than he had intended. John Allan was gone. Mr. Royster was gone. No one and nothing could separate them now. For those three months, Edgar did not drink. He came alive again. But too soon the time came for him to return to New York. Once he had launched his new magazine, he would return to Richmond and Elmira.

On the night he was to leave, Elmira confessed, "I never knew until later that Father had destroyed your letters. I thought you had abandoned me." Elmira sighed deeply. "I loved you once and you left. Now you are leaving again."

Edgar had booked passage on a steamer bound from Norfolk, Virginia, to Baltimore. From there he would board a train for New York City and then close the deal on his magazine. "Once you gave me your word that you would marry me," Edgar said.

"That was long ago. We were children," she said.

"Will you give me your word now?"

Elmira fondly smoothed a lock of black hair from Edgar's forehead, then suddenly looked alarmed. "You're feverish." She pressed her fingertips against his chest. "Your heart races."

"It is some illness, nothing serious," he assured her.

"Do not travel to Norfolk tonight, Edgar. You are not well."

He closed his hand over hers. "I fear leaving you," he admitted. "I have such a cold feeling that I shall never see you again."

"Then stay. Please stay."

He kissed her hand. "I promised you that I would be a man of letters. Now I must go to New York City and take care of this business. When I return, you will be waiting for me?"

Elmira did not answer. Reluctantly he walked away.

"Edgar?" she called after him suddenly. "I married another man, but the love of my life was you. I never loved anyone but you."

The words were spoken too late. He had already gone and did not hear.

The steamer departed Norfolk as scheduled. The next morning in a heavy rain, the ship docked at Baltimore. Poe stepped onto the wharf and . . . entered the labyrinth again. What happened in those dark passages over the next few days no one knows for certain.

"Edgar Poe! Is that you? Rotten weather but what good luck to meet up with you! Come, I'll buy you a drink."

Edgar stared at the man and then remembered. "You were at the university."

"You were quite the scholar. Here's a tavern. Let's drink to old times."

Edgar shook his head. "I must board a train for New York City. I've an appointment—"

"Haven't you heard?" the man said. "The weather has delayed everything all round. The train won't leave for hours." He drew Edgar toward the tavern door.

Edgar rubbed his hot forehead. "I don't think . . ."

"Why, you're shivering like a wet cat," the man said. "A brandy will warm you and clear your head."

Edgar protested but then reconsidered. "Perhaps just one."

The man guided him into the tavern and out of the rain. The air was thick with smoke. It swirled and took shapes of all the frightening things in Edgar's dreams. He reeled. "I must get back to the steamer."

"The steamer? I thought it was a train you were taking?" The man pulled out a chair. "What is your hurry?"

A week later, neither Muddy in New York City nor Elmira in Richmond had heard from Edgar. In Baltimore, however, Dr. Joseph Snodgrass received a curious letter. *There is a gentleman,* it read, *rather the worse for wear, at Ryan's 4th ward tavern who goes under the name of Edgar A. Poe and who appears in great distress & says he is acquainted with you. I assure you, he is in need of immediate assistance.*

Dr. Snodgrass stared at the letter. Years ago when Poe lived in the attic garret with Maria Clemm, he had himself encouraged the young man's writing career. Years had passed, and he had heard little more of him. The doctor made his way to Ryan's tavern. The man in question looked nothing like the poet the doctor remembered. He was wearing cheap, filthy clothes that were clearly not his own. And yet, he clutched a fancy, carved wooden cane. Edgar's face was haggard; his hair, unwashed. He was utterly stupefied with liquor. And yet, as Snodgrass examined him closer, he feared the man suffered from an illness and not just drunkenness.

"What has happened to you? Where have you been?" the doctor questioned him, but Poe was unable to walk or speak clearly.

The doctor took him to Washington College Hospital. In a grim, prisonlike room with barred windows, Poe lay delirious in his bed. His arms and leg shook. At times, he shouted at the imaginary creatures he saw in the room. The doctors could do little to help him except bathe him and try to keep him comfortable.

On the evening of October 7, Dr. Snodgrass composed a letter to Maria Clemm. He weighed how much he should reveal. He remembered that Maria was a loving aunt. Reluctantly, he wrote:

I discovered him in this critical condition, delirious, wearing filthy clothes that were obviously not his. His condition was so deteriorated that I could do nothing for him. In his final hours, he became quiet and seemed to rest. His final words were "Lord, help my poor soul." My sympathy to you, Madam.

Edgar Poe was buried in Baltimore. The service lasted no longer than three minutes, for the weather was still raw and wet. Only a few mourners stood over the fresh grave: among them, an old gentleman named Master Clark and an attorney, Z. Collins Lee, who told the grave digger he knew the poet as a friend in his youth.

No one else came to grieve. Edgar Poe died as he had lived and loved—alone.

The Mountain Lion

From the novel by Jean Stafford

MOLLY WAS DIFFERENT FROM OTHER PEOPLE. WHAT
RALPH DID NOT REALIZE WAS HOW TIGHTLY
INTERTWINED HIS LIFE HAD BECOME WITH HERS.

*U*ncle Claude put his hand on Ralph's shoulder and said, "I'm mighty glad you've come to stay awhile this time." Ralph, while he did not pull away, felt himself grow cold with something like distrust for the enthusiasm in his uncle's voice, so boylike that it actually cracked.

"Don't you know how I've always said I wanted to get me a mountain lion?" Uncle Claude said. "Well, I'm on the trail of one now."

Ralph could not make up his mind about his uncle. One thing was certain—he was not as nice as Grandpa had been. When Ralph and his sister, Molly, made small mistakes, Uncle Claude always laughed at them and told about them at the table. Once when Molly was younger, she'd asked who milked all the cattle on the range, and Uncle Claude had laughed so hard he made her cry. That was years ago during earlier visits to their uncle's ranch in the mountains. Now, at sixteen, Ralph had come to stay for the entire year while his parents traveled around the world. Molly had come too, but she wasn't very happy about it either.

Uncle Claude was waiting to be questioned about the lion, and Ralph now asked, "Where did you see it?"

He had seen her only once, he said, in early April in the foothills near Garland Peak. He had gone back time after time to have another glimpse of her or of her mate. He wanted her hide so much that he had wasted a lot of hunting time just fooling around looking for her and hadn't gotten a piece of game this year, though there was plenty to be had. She was about as big as a good-sized dog, Uncle Claude said, and she looked for all the world like an overgrown house cat. He thought about her so much that he had given her a name. He called her Goldilocks because, running the way she had in the sunlight, she had been as blond as a movie star.

Uncle Claude had told the boys who worked for him that he would fire any of them who drew a bead on the lion—if anyone got her, it was going to be him. No one had quite understood why Uncle Claude was so all-fired crazy to get her, and he could not quite make it out himself.

"I've decided to let you hunt her too, Ralph," he said. But Ralph was never to hunt alone. And when they hunted together, they were to keep within hailing distance of each other.

This special honor made Ralph feel as if he were actually rising in the air and improved the outlook for his year-long stay. Ralph warmly thanked Uncle Claude. At the same time, deceitfully and unsportingly, he resolved that it would be *he*, not the man, who got the lion.

Molly would not learn to shoot, and she did not like to touch a gun, even when it was unloaded. Her mother had frequently warned her that unloaded guns were always the ones that went off. Throughout that fall and winter, Molly would go alone on Saturday mornings up to the summit of Garland Peak. She went when the autumn aspens shone like money among the conifers on all the foothills and the high fields were dark green with the first shoots of winter wheat. She went even on the coldest days, when the snow-drifts were deep and the pine needles in the glades were solid with ice. The shapes of the high blue trees were hidden by the snow that loaded their branches, and they looked like formless ghosts. Sometimes the wind came fiercely down the trackless slopes, blowing sharp pellets into her face.

It seemed to Molly, when she was alone in the mountains, that she had been by herself for years now, ever since Grandpa had died. It was as if Ralph and her mother and father were no blood kin to her at all anymore, as if nobody ever had been except Grandpa. She kept to herself at school, which she disliked this year. She disliked the harsh mountain voices of the students and the teachers and the smell of winter clothes. The others in her grade were so backward that Molly had to be given extra work to occupy her.

The only things that really gave her pleasure were the hibernating ladybugs she sometimes found under rocks, the stories she wrote, and the mountains. Here she did not think about her yellow skin covered by hundreds of shining bronze freckles. At 14, Molly felt that she had a homemade look, as if she had been put together by an inexperienced hand.

Every Saturday, she took her camera along to the mountains. She hoped that she would one day see Goldilocks and snap her photograph. In earlier summers, Ralph had gone along on these mountain hikes. They had often seen deer grazing among the blue flowers. But this year—alone—she had not yet seen a wild animal, not even a rabbit.

On the Saturday before Christmas, Uncle Claude decided he and Ralph should go into the mountains with Molly to cut down a Christmas tree. There had been a big snowfall on Thursday. The sun was warm on the slopes and brilliant in the branches of the evergreens. The climb was easy and the path was deep in snow so that they made no sound. Once Molly broke off an ice-covered twig on a chokecherry bush, but the noise was slight.

Uncle Claude was the first to get to the opposite bank of the gulch. Now he moved into the cover of a small scrub oak loaded with snow, and he motioned for Ralph and Molly to join him. They stepped carefully in his bootprints, not seeing yet what he did. Then, when they were beside him, he pointed.

The mountain lion was standing still with her head up, her long tail twitching. She was honey-colored all over save for her face, which was darker, a sort of yellow-brown. She allowed them to look at her for only a few seconds, and then she bounded across the place where the columbines grew in summer and disappeared among the trees. Her flight was lovely—her wasteless grace and her speed did not make Molly think immediately of fear but of power.

"This *would* be the day we'd see her, when we didn't bring our guns," said Uncle Claude. His face did not show disappointment as much as anger, as if he really hated the mountain lion and wanted to kill her for spite and not for sport.

Ralph did not say a word but continued to look at the place where she had been, smiling a great secret smile. Molly was afraid and thought she could never come here again. She imagined its claws, its teeth, the way it would hiss. When they again started down the mountain, pulling the just-chopped tree on a sled, Molly twice looked back over her shoulder, and she kept close to Ralph. When they got home, she went straight into the house, feeling unsafe until then.

That night, nibbling at an apple in front of the fire, Molly told the housekeeper, "We saw Goldilocks today." Molly saw fear arrive in the woman's face and stay there. "A mountain lion isn't dangerous," said Molly, courageous in the presence of this adult cowardice. "They're just as afraid of people as deer are."

"Perhaps," said the woman. "But I'll feel safer when it's dead. I hope you will not go back there. It's not right for a girl to be alone out there with a lion loose."

It seemed to Molly then that Ralph and Uncle Claude had gone to the mountains with her deliberately, knowing they would see the mountain lion. It was the only place she was happy being Molly, but Goldilocks and her uncle and Ralph, too, had ruined everything. Molly threw her apple core into the fire and heard it hiss briefly. She, too, would not feel safe until the beautiful animal was dead.

In the weeks and months that followed, Ralph dreamed of the mountain lion and thought, "Oh, if I don't get her, I will *die!*"

He saw himself standing where they had stood before Christmas, taking perfect aim, shooting her through her proud head with its wary eyes and then running across the mesa to stroke her soft golden flanks and paws. Ralph had decided he would not skin the mountain lion, but would have her stuffed and keep her in his room all his life. If he had to go to college, he would take her along with him.

He felt, somehow, that he had a right to Goldilocks. He wanted her because he loved her, but Uncle Claude wanted her only because she was something rare.

On Easter Sunday, they saw Goldilocks again. This time she was beside the stream, nearer the gulch than the place where she had vanished before, close to the beaver dam. They had only a brief glimpse of her before she leaped away and was gone before they could even raise their rifles.

They ran to the place where she had been and found that she had left her food, too startled by their voices to carry it off. A half-eaten woodchuck lay beside a tree stump, its entrails chewed but its head intact and twisted to an awkward angle. The animal had been mauled and slobbered on, and its grizzled hair was clotted. Blood was now on some of the wood chips left by the beavers when they had gnawed down the tree.

Frustrated and angry, Uncle Claude moved around the stump, examining everything as if he expected to find a clue that would lead him to her den. Sighing, he said, "Blast the yellow beast."

And Ralph, feeling himself on the verge of tears, said desolately, "What'll we do now?"

"Go home, I reckon," said Uncle Claude, "but I'm going to get me my cat yet."

Ralph kept the edge out of his voice when he said, "You mean, I'm going to get me *my* cat."

Uncle Claude glanced sidelong at him but said nothing, and they started down the creek bank. The creek was swollen from the thaws, and there were places where the water sprayed like a geyser in the hollows between the rocks. Between two boulders at a widening, Ralph saw the points of a set of antlers sticking up out of the water, and he waded in, not bothering to take off his shoes.

What he found was not just one set of antlers. He found the skulls of two deer with horns so tightly interlocked that he could not get them apart. They were wedged in between the rocks, and he had trouble getting them loose. The water was cold and flicked up his pants legs. Once he lost his footing and slipped on a rock.

When he came out with his trophy, he found Uncle Claude sitting on a patch of grass, watching Ralph. "What'll you do with them now you got them?" he asked.

Ralph did not answer but tried again to get the horns apart. His heart constricted when he imagined what must have taken place—the two bucks charging each other and then, by lunatic accident, being joined as one, toppling into the water to drown, still struggling to get free. It was not so much the violence of this wilderness death that made Ralph quiver. It was his uncle's indifference, the same cold calm he had when he spoke of killing Goldilocks.

"What'll you do with the antlers?" Uncle Claude repeated.

"I'll take them to Molly."

Uncle Claude laughed shortly. "You'd better take Molly a box of candy to sweeten her disposition. What's the matter with that kid anyway?"

Ralph took in his breath sharply. "Search me," he said.

Molly was just different from other people, he supposed. When she took off her glasses she looked like a big-eyed rabbit. He liked her when they were alone, but she embarrassed him in public because she said or did such weird things. When he was eight, she'd decided she was going to be kidnapped and had worn a Halloween mask on the school bus every day for a whole month.

Later that same year, they'd both had scarlet fever. After that, they had always been together. There was only one thing about Molly that Ralph had not liked and that was the way she used to copy him. He would finish telling a joke, and right away she would repeat exactly what he had said so that there was no time for people to laugh. Not only that, but she had countless times told his dreams, pretending that they were her own.

When Ralph was younger, he had often looked at his weedy sister with dislike. Sometimes he had wanted to cry out with despair because her love was really the only one he had except for Grandpa's, and he found it nothing but a burden and a bother. She had kept a diary in which she recorded everything he said and everything he did, and she insisted on reading each entry to him before they went to bed. At first he had been flattered, but later he was only embarrassed.

Now she no longer read to him from her diary. She hardly spoke to him at all and when she did, it was with scorn. She called him fat, though he wasn't. He remembered, though, how he and Molly had sobbed silently together for Grandpa on the floor beside his coffin. Nothing had ever been really right since Grandpa had died.

Later, when Ralph took the locked antlers up to Molly's room, she stared at his present with terrible woe but without scorn. For the first time in a long time, a look of understanding passed between them. "Thanks, Ralph," she said.

Finally it was spring and school was over. On the night of Molly's eighth-grade commencement, Ralph sat in the hot auditorium where the June bugs bumbled foolishly against the window screens. He was clutched by terror at the shortness of time. He knew that his parents, who were now in Venice, would soon return, and there was no time to lose, for he *must* have Goldilocks before they came.

Molly was sitting three rows away from him, and she turned around and looked directly at her brother, puffing out her cheeks to look like a fat person. Ralph frowned. How wrong he had been the day he had given her the antlers and had thought they understood each other again. Molly, Ralph decided, did not want to be happy. What was worse, she wanted him to be as wretched as she was.

The next day, Ralph took his rifle up to Garland Peak. Uncle Claude had taken a mare to stud, and he told Ralph that when he got through, he would come looking for him in the hills. Ralph knew he couldn't shoot until Uncle Claude came, but still he hunted.

He moved around the beaver dam, looking alertly through the trees. Just beyond this black silent pool was a little glade with a large flat rock in the center. He thought he heard someone across the dam and stopped to listen, but he decided that the sound had only been a bird rustling. The thought came to him that Uncle Claude might have made the noise, but then he decided that the man could not have returned from the stud farm so soon.

Quiet as it was, Ralph had a feeling, as always in the forest, of life nearby. And when, softly moving aside a branch of chokecherry, he saw Goldilocks in the glade beside the flat rock, he was not surprised. He had been certain, in this last moment, that he would find her there.

She was feeding on a jackrabbit. Delicately she moved the rabbit with her paw and then savagely ripped it with her teeth. He stood, holding his breath, utterly motionless for a minute, debating, but he could not hold out against the temptation. Uncle Claude would have to forgive him, and if he didn't, Ralph was going away soon anyway.

As he raised his rifle, Ralph heard another sound, but this time from the direction of the face of the mountain. Goldilocks heard it too and lifted her heavy head. Before she could find him with her topaz eyes, Ralph shot and immediately he was stone blind. His blindness lasted for an exploded moment, and when he was able to see again, to see the tumbled yellow body on the bright grass, he realized that he had been not blind but deaf, for there had been another gun, another shot a split second after his.

Uncle Claude came charging through the brush, hollering. "We done it! We both done it!"

He ran to the lion, throwing his gun on the ground. She had fallen toward Ralph on her wounded side, and no blood was visible. Uncle Claude turned her over to look for the wounds, and Ralph stepped forward.

"She's so little," said Ralph softly, as if Goldilocks were not dead but only asleep. "Why, she isn't any bigger than a dog. She isn't as *big*."

But what mattered was whose bullet had killed her. They looked eagerly, pushing back the hair with their hands. Ralph was surprised to see how short and harsh it was. There was only one bullet hole, and it was not in the place where Ralph had aimed. He was sick with failure, sick and furious with his uncle for coming so quietly and winning so easily.

Uncle Claude said, "No man alive can judge which one of us got her, I reckon. We'll have to call it a corporation."

There was a sound in the chokecherry bushes beyond them, opposite where Ralph had stood to shoot. It was a sound that could come only from a human throat. It was a bubbling of blood. Uncle Claude and Ralph stood up and looked at each other in an agony of terror. For a moment they could not move but stood, hatless, the sun blazing down upon them and upon the lion at their feet.

"Somebody . . ."

Uncle Claude, bending almost in two at the waist, ran across the clearing, and Ralph followed, his body a flame of pain. Molly lay beside a rotten log, a wound like a burst fruit in her forehead. Her glasses lay in fragments on her cheeks, and the frame, torn from one ear, stuck up at a raffish angle. The sound in her throat stopped. Uncle Claude knelt down beside her, but Ralph stood some paces away. He could as clearly see the life leave her as you could see fire leave burned-out wood. It receded like a tide, lifted like a fog.

When Uncle Claude stood up, Ralph began to scream. He threw back his head and with his mouth as wide as it would open, he let the sound flow out of him, burning up the mountains. Then he was too hoarse to scream any longer, and he threw himself down on the ground and pounded the pine needles with his fists and with his feet, moaning, "I didn't see her! I didn't hear her! I didn't kill her!"

"I know *that*," Uncle Claude said sharply. "Shove, now. Go on. *Get* somebody."

In a minute, Ralph thought, just let me have a minute. He knelt down beside his sister and touched the blood on her forehead, stroked her cheeks, felt her sodden hair. "Molly," he said. "Molly girl."

Uncle Claude kicked him in the ribs and said, "When I say shove, I mean shove!"

He had to go then. He stumbled across the clearing trying not to look at Goldilocks. "Molly, Molly, Molly, Molly," he muttered like a crazy man.

By the time help came and they got Molly down to the car, the sun was setting. They had tied a handkerchief around her forehead so that you could not see the hole, but the blood had soaked through. Uncle Claude sat in the front, and Ralph sat in the back beside Molly.

There was neither a past nor a future to his life in this single, yellow minute. He looked straight ahead, watching the road being devoured by the car.

PART II

The Outcasts

The Chameleon

by Jordan Phillips

THEY TOLD HIM HE WAS NO GOOD.
MITCH BELIEVED THEM . . . UNTIL HE MET ADAM.

"You ain't nothin'," the kid wearing the red bandanna says. "You ain't nobody."

He presses a piece of pipe against Mitch's chest so hard that Mitch can feel the metal through the thickness of his L.A. Raiders jacket.

Mitch turns to stone. He wills his eyes to go cold and hard so that the red bandanna can't see what Mitch is feeling inside. He has a brick wall behind him, a wall of Coyotes in front of him, and nowhere to run.

"Zero, that's you, man," says the red bandanna, "tryin' to make a dollar out of 15 cents." He laughs. The others laugh, too. Then, just like that, the red bandanna tosses the pipe on the ground and walks away. The others follow.

Mitch wants to believe that it is his stone-cold face that has defeated them, but he knows it is because they got what they wanted—to humiliate a Python on his own turf.

The street is empty now. The Coyotes are gone, but Mitch is still shaking inside. He knows what a pipe can do to the side of a kid's head. Mitch walks past empty buildings and storefronts with metal cages over the windows. By the time he reaches the house where he lives with his brother, anger has begun to coil inside him, replacing the fear.

No one is home. Mitch goes into his brother's bedroom. In the top drawer, he finds the handgun.

Mitch is a Python. And a Python always strikes back.

Three months later, Mitch stands beside his older brother Jerry in a courtroom. Jerry is Mitch's legal guardian. This is Mitch's second court appearance. Judge Carmichael has seen a hundred Mitches before—some older, some younger. They wear different colors for different gangs, but they are all the same. This one is fifteen, and he has just completed serving three months in a youth camp for a gang shooting.

"The boy you shot may never walk again," the judge speaks, looking down at his papers and not at Mitch. "Do you have any idea what that means, Mitchell, not to walk again?"

"I didn't mean to hurt anyone," Mitch answers sullenly. Even *he* doesn't believe it.

"You entered a rival gang's neighborhood with a gun and fired into a crowd of people, but you didn't mean to hurt anyone? Just what did you 'mean' to do?"

Mitch doesn't tell him about the pipe and the brick wall and being jumped by a gang of Coyotes.

"Well, Mitchell?" The judge looks up at last, expecting a reply. "What were you thinking when you took that gun from your brother's house?"

"I just wanted to . . . scare them," he said.

The judge leans forward. "Do you know right from wrong, Mitchell?"

Mitch cocks his chin. His voice is cold. "Yes, I know right from wrong."

"And what you did, Mitchell, was that right or wrong?"

He hates the way the judge is talking down to him, like he really is a zero. Mitch shifts his feet, then rolls his shoulders. He decides not to answer. The judge sits back. He passes judgment: probation until the age of twenty-five.

"Ten years?" Jerry says, speaking for the first time. "He's already served three months. He's just a kid."

"No, he is a felon." Judge Carmichael continues. "I've assigned him a probation officer. He will find an alternative school where Mitchell will study and do community service. I'm recommending the Wheeler School."

The name means nothing to Mitch. The judge explains. Wheeler is a school for severely handicapped children. If they accept Mitchell, then the judge will not send him back to the youth camp.

"Handicapped?" Mitch repeats. "You mean retarded kids? Kids in wheelchairs?"

The judge nods solemnly. "Perhaps when I see you in another three months, you'll know what it means to be unable to walk."

Two days later, Mitch is sitting in the principal's office at the Wheeler School. With him is his probation officer. The head teacher is Janet Willis. She has a stern look on her face. Mitch knows that she does not like him. Mitch shoves his hands into the pockets of his Raiders jacket, looking away as she speaks. "No one is going to make you come to our school, Mitch. It will be your decision," she says.

"Some choice. Hang here with a bunch of rejects or go back to jail." They may call it a youth camp, but it was still jail.

"Oh, you won't be hanging out, Mitch. You'll take care of the children. That is, *if* we decide to accept you."

"I thought you said it was *my* choice."

Now the principal takes a turn. "What Janet is trying to say, Mitch, is we have to be convinced that you want to change. Unless you want to change, there is nothing we or anyone else can do for you."

He narrows his eyes. "Caring for them how?"

"On the street, it's hands-off. But in here, it's hands-on. You'll have to feed them, groom them, help some to learn how to walk again. Do you think you can handle that?"

He shrugs. But inside he is all stone and ice. "Yeah, sure."

Janet glances doubtfully at the principal. Mitch recognizes the look. He's seen it lots of times—from his brother, the kid wearing the red bandanna, Judge Carmichael. It says "You're nobody; a zero."

Mitch's probation officer states the rules Mitch must follow if he comes to Wheeler. One, he must attend school every day. Two, he must be in his brother's house by nine o'clock. "Every night," the probation officer emphasizes.

"For ten years?"

"It's called probation, Mitch," he says, then continues. Three, he must make all court appearances. Four, he must not break any laws, including fighting of any kind.

Janet Willis adds one more. "Five, give up the jacket. Gang symbols aren't allowed in this school." She holds out her hand, waiting.

She and Mitch stare at one another. The jacket is Mitch's protection on the streets. It tells everyone who he is—a Python.

"The jacket, Mitch, or this interview ends right now." Mitch looks away. He takes off the jacket.

Mitch steps outside the office and waits with his probation officer. Behind the principal's closed door Janet Willis makes her objections quite clear. "He *shot* somebody. Our kids can't protect themselves from him."

The principal smiles. "They may be in wheelchairs, Janet, but you know they aren't powerless. I've a feeling they'll do more for Mitch Ryan than he does for them."

Janet shakes her head, unconvinced. "Why don't we wait until Luis comes back with *his* report," she suggests.

Luis is a former gang member. Now he is a teacher's aide at the school. He takes Mitch on a tour of the building, leading him to the cafeteria first. Before entering, Luis suddenly turns on Mitch. "What gang you run with?"

"Pythons."

"Yeah?" Luis steps closer. His face is an inch from Mitch's. "I hate Pythons."

Mitch feels it again, fear sucking the warmth out of him. He does what he has learned to do—turn to stone. He looks down the hall to the principal's closed door and thinks, *They're setting me up. It was all a bunch of crap what they said in there about wanting to change.*

"You want to hit me, don't you?" Luis said.

"One punch and I'm back in youth camp. You know that."

"So?" Luis taunts him. "You don't want to come here anyway, do you, Mitchell? Hangin' out with a bunch of rejects?"

"Look, can we just get on with this tour?"

"I'm going to tell you something, Mitchell. You're no Python now. You're a chameleon. Do you know what a chameleon is, Mitchell?"

There it is again, that same put-down tone of voice. But Mitch doesn't know what a chameleon is. He shakes his head.

"A lizard. Colors don't mean nothing to a chameleon, because it changes colors. It fits in. That's you, Mitchell. This is a whole new situation here, and you've got to change your colors to fit in. Understand?"

Mitch nods. Luis steps back and pushes open the door to the cafeteria.

Later, Luis meets privately with the principal and Janet Willis. "He's OK. I pressed him a bit, but he didn't come back at me. I don't think he'll hurt anybody."

"Well, Janet?" the principal asks.

She shakes her head and sighs. "Fine. I'll give him a chance."

On Monday morning, yellow school buses pull into the parking lot. Mitch watches as an elevator platform lowers the first student in a wheelchair to ground level. "Are they . . . you know, all there?"

"Some have learning problems, yes," Janet says. "But that doesn't mean they aren't all there.'"

She nods to a teenage girl with a cane whom Luis is leading up the ramp and into the school. She and Luis are laughing. The girl's name is Carla, Janet says. She's blind. Now Janet smiles at a five-year-old boy who steps off the bus. "That's Brian. He's autistic."

"What's that? Something contagious?"

Janet laughs. "No, it's a kind of emotional problem. He doesn't talk much or play with other children." Janet looks closer at Mitch. "You aren't afraid of disabled people, are you, Mitch?"

"Me? No. Why should I be afraid of them?"

"Good. Then why don't you help Adam into the school, then?"

A boy about Mitch's age waits in a wheelchair.

"What's wrong with him?" Mitch asks.

"He has cerebral palsy. He knows what he wants to do," Janet explains. "He just can't get his muscles to do it. I'm thinking Adam is a little bit like you," she says.

Mitch doesn't move. Maybe this was a mistake. Maybe the youth camp was the better choice.

"Well, go on, Mitch. Adam's waiting." Janet walks away, leaving him on his own.

"You've got to prove yourself to join a gang, man," Mitch says. "You've got to show them that you can take whatever bad stuff they throw at you."

It is noon. Mitch is feeding Adam. Because of his disability, the muscles in his right arm jerk. Mitch guides a spoon of rice from the plate to Adam's mouth. Adam swallows. A few grains of rice stick to his chin.

The tinny echo of music comes from the Walkman earphones that hang around Mitch's neck. When Adam reaches for the earphones, Mitch recoils. "Hands off. This is my property."

"What . . . trouble got you here?" Adam asks. He talks slowly and with some difficulty.

"It was stupid."

"Stupid to get caught," Adam says.

"It's a hard world out there. But you wouldn't know anything about that."

Adam reaches for the spoon, wanting to feed himself. But his hand jerks involuntarily, and the rice spills onto Mitch's lap. Adam mutters, scolding himself, "Stupid. Stupid." Frustrated, he sweeps the tray of food off the table. It splatters onto the floor.

Across the room, Luis turns and looks. Mitch knows Luis doesn't think he can do this. Mitch isn't sure he can either. He takes a napkin and wipes the rice from Adam's mouth. "Don't ever say that. Don't ever let *anybody* tell you that."

Mitch gets a clean spoon and another dish. But Adam presses his lips together and shakes his head. "Yeah," Mitch says, "you're right. The food here *is* pretty crappy."

Mitch sticks his finger in his mouth as if to gag himself. Adam grins.

"So what do you say?" Mitch teases. "After lunch, let's

jog across town and check out some babes. Or would you
rather just, you know, shoot some hoops?"

Adam laughs. His head bobs with palsy, but also with
laughter. He takes the food Mitch offers and eats again.

Each morning, Mitch works with the disabled children.
Each afternoon, he attends a class taught by Janet. Some
of the disabled children are also in the class. Most are
younger than Mitch. On the first day, Janet gives him a
journal and tells him to write down what he notices about
the kids at Wheeler and about himself. "You going to read
it?" he asks.

"If you don't want me to read it, then just fold the
page over, like this," she shows him. "I'll respect your pri-
vacy."

His first journal entry reads: *They're like babies. Even
Adam. He trusts me. The fastest way to get yourself hurt is to
trust somebody.* He doesn't bother to fold the page.

On the fifth day, he writes: *What I like best about
working with Adam is making him laugh. When he comes off
the bus, he looks for me now. He won't let anybody else feed
him but me. He thinks I'm his friend.* Again he doesn't fold
the page. Let her read it. He doesn't care.

At the end of two weeks, Mitch writes: *There's one
problem with this place—it's closed on weekends.* It is only a
single sentence, but after a moment, Mitch creases the
page and closes the book.

At noon on the Monday of Mitch's fourth week, while the
others are eating in the cafeteria, Mitch wheels Adam out
a side door. Janet doesn't realize Mitch is gone until he

doesn't show up for her afternoon class. She is angry, but her anger turns to apprehension when Luis tells her that Adam is also missing.

"They can't have gone too far with one boy in a wheelchair," Luis reasons. "I can take the van and go cruisin' for them. I know a couple of places Mitch might have taken him."

"Or we can call the police," Janet says.

"The police?" Luis says.

"Well, this is a violation of his probation, not just school rules."

The principal has listened quietly to the conversation. She prefers to let her teachers voice their opinions rather than commanding them to do as she bids. Now she opens her desk drawer and hands Luis the keys to the school van. "You have one hour to find them, Luis," she says. "Then we call the police."

At the Burger Barn, Adam is eating fries by himself, using his fingers. Around his neck are Mitch's earphones. "I've been thinking," Mitch tells him. "The reason why you can't walk so great is 'cause you've got the wrong sneakers."

Adam laughs. His head bobs.

"No, really. We need to get you some Air Jordans. Costs lots of dough, but you'll see the difference on the court."

Four boys enter the restaurant and sit at a table across the room. They notice Adam right away. "Hey," one shouts at Mitch. "What's wrong with him?"

Mitch looks down at the fries on the table. He takes a napkin and wipes Adam's fingers. "Time to go."

"Why, Mitch?"

They don't recognize him, yet. He is not wearing the Raiders jacket because Janet forbids it. Mitch stands, keeping his back to them.

"Hey, we asked you a question. What's wrong with that jerk?"

He pulls Adam's wheelchair away from the table. He hears a chair squeak and knows they are standing up, too.

"Who are they?" Adam asks.

Mitch turns the chair around, facing the door. Even as he pushes Adam forward, he feels a hand grip his shoulder, stopping him. Two others step alongside the chair. Just as Mitch feared, their eyes light up as they see whom they've trapped. "*You!* You're the one."

Mitch sees, too late, that Adam's seat belt is not buckled. But he has no choice. He pushes past the Coyotes and through the door. He eases Adam off the curb and starts walking fast across the parking lot. But of course, they can easily outrun a wheelchair. In the parking lot, the Coyotes surround him.

"You," the tall one says. He slams the palm of his hand against Mitch's shoulder, shoving him back, but Mitch does not let go of the wheelchair.

Mitch bluffs. "Four of you and two of us? Don't make my buddy here get out of his chair. That'll really tick him off."

"Two of you?" the tall one laughs. "One and a half of you. No, one and a fourth."

"Who are they, Mitch?" Adam asks again.

"Tell him who we are, Mitch. Friends of Jeff Davies."

Mitch has two choices. He can leave Adam and run.

Or he could stay and fight. If he runs, Adam is helpless. If he fights, the judge will send him back to youth camp. Either way, he loses.

One of the Coyotes makes the decision for him. He grabs the earphones from Adam's neck. "Give them back!" Adam shouts. He reaches up, but his arm shakes with the palsy. Two of the Coyotes mock him. They twist their mouths and curl their fingers into claws and moan. "Give them back!" Adam shouts louder. Drool is in the corner of his mouth. Mitch looks over his shoulder at the windows of the Burger Barn. Doesn't anyone inside see what's happening?

"Is this retard your friend?" a Coyote asks Mitch.

"He's not a retard, and yeah, he's my friend."

"Jeff Davies was my friend," the tall one says. "And you shot him."

Adam twists to look up at Mitch. "You . . . shot someone?"

"It was a mistake. A bad mistake."

"You got that right," the tall one says. He pulls a knife from somewhere inside his jacket and waves it in front of Mitch. He presses it against Mitch's chest. At the same time, the others yank the wheelchair forward, out of Mitch's hands. They wheel the chair around and around. Mitch steps forward, but the knife presses harder. "I've been looking for you a long time."

The Coyotes charge across the parking lot, bouncing the wheelchair over the speed bumps. Mitch sees Adam's ragdoll legs dragging on the pavement.

"OK, OK," Mitch says. "So you found me. Just don't hurt Adam."

"Why not? You hurt my friend. You hurt him real bad. Eye for an eye."

"But he didn't do anything to you!" Mitch pleads.

The Coyotes dump Adam's chair. Unable to brace himself, Adam pitches forward. The door of the restaurant swings open, and the manager comes outside, shouting. A second later, the first wails of a police car echo down the street. And just like that, the knife disappears again into the folds of the jacket.

The tall one grins. "You!" he says, pointing. "I'm coming back for you. I don't forget you." And then the Coyotes run. A van swerves into the parking lot. One of the Coyotes bounces off the side of the van, then twists away, and is gone.

Mitch goes to Adam. His lip is split and bleeding. Mitch tries to lift him back into the chair, but Adam curls up on his side, refusing to cooperate. "Go away," Adam says, shaking.

Alone in the principal's office, Mitch waits for his probation officer. The feeling is back in his stomach—the stones and ice he had the day the kid in the red bandanna slammed him against a wall and pressed a pipe to his chest. Someone is always pressing something against his throat. They'll send him back to the youth camp, he knows. But that isn't what scares him.

The door opens. Janet comes into the room and closes the door behind her.

"Is Adam OK?"

She nods. "Why did you do it?"

He shrugs. "He's a kid. Like me."

"And?" she prompts.

"And he needs to have some fun. He needs some friends."

"Not your kind of fun, Mitch. Not your kind of friends."

He turns on her. "No, you're wrong. Adam needs me!"

"I thought so too, until today."

"You can't kick me out," he says, but so quietly that Janet isn't quite sure what he has said.

"What?"

"I'm sorry about what happened. I want to stay here."

"I see. Well, that's not good enough." She walks to the door.

Mitch shouts, "Yeah, well, go ahead, then. Send me back. That's how it always is. I'm never good enough. I'm nobody." His voice cracks. "I'm zero."

Janet removes her hand from the doorknob. "I never said that about you."

"You didn't have to. I see it in the way you look at me. You and Luis. Except . . . I'm not a zero. Not anymore. That's why I have to stay here."

Janet crosses her arms. "How is Wheeler different from anywhere else?"

He doesn't know. "Maybe," he says, "it's Adam. He needs me. Nobody ever needed me before."

She smiles. "It's a good feeling, isn't it?"

Mitch looks at her. "Give me a second chance, Janet. I can be like that lizard thing Luis says I should be."

"What lizard thing?"

"The chameleon. The one that changes color."

"Luis said that?"

"I can be more like him, like Luis. I just need a little more time."

Janet opens the door. "There is someone here to see you."

Mitch rubs his hands over his face. When he looks up again, he expects to see his probation officer. But Adam is there in his wheelchair. His lip is badly swollen and bruised. He doesn't smile. Suddenly Mitch realizes that he has gotten it all wrong. Adam doesn't need him. He needs Adam.

"They were after me, not you," he tells him. "They knew they could hurt me by hurting you."

"Who . . . did you kill?"

"Oh, no! I didn't kill anybody," Mitch says. "I was lucky, though, because I could have." Mitch sits down so that he can look at Adam face to face. "I put him in a wheelchair, maybe for life."

"That's why they sent you here," Adam says.

"You're not the one who needs help." Mitch laughs. "Funny, isn't it? I mean, look at you. Look at me. You're OK. I'm not so great."

Janet puts her hand on Adam's shoulder. "If Adam says you stay, then I won't object."

Mitch looks at him. "Friends have to stick together, don't they, Adam?"

Slowly, he smiles. "You can't go yet. Mitch. I still need . . . new sneakers."

Mitch grins. Then he reaches for Adam's limp hand and squeezes.

A Man Called Horse

by Dorothy M. Johnson

*THE YOUNG MAN FROM BOSTON WISHED TO BE THE
EQUAL OF OTHER MEN, BUT FIRST HE HAD TO LIVE AS A SLAVE.*

He was a young man of good family in the New
England of a hundred-odd years ago, and the reasons for his bitter discontent were unclear, even to himself.
He grew up in the gracious old Boston home under his
grandmother's care. His mother had died early, but he had
always known the comfort and privilege of his father's
wealth.

The discontent puzzled him because he could not
define it. He wanted to live among equals—people who
were no better than he and no worse either. That was as
close as he could come to describing the source of his
unhappiness and his restless desire to go somewhere else.
He had the idea that in Indian country, where there was
danger, all white men were kings, and he wanted to be one
of them.

And so, in the year 1845 he left home and went out West, far beyond the country's creeping frontier. Because he had money, he could afford to hire friends. Four men cooked and hunted and served as his guides through the wilderness, but they were not very friendly. They were apart from him, and he was still alone. He still brooded about his status in the world.

On a day in June he learned what it was to have no status at all. While he was unarmed and bathing in a creek, a raiding party of Crow Indians captured him. He heard gunfire and the brief shouts of his companions around the bend of the creek, just before they died. He had no chance to fight.

His captors let him run. And they gave chase, for sport. They struck him with the sticks that carried the dripping scalps of his companions. Then they took him along in a matter-of-fact way, as they took the horses they captured. Like the horses, the white man was unshod. Like those animals, too, he wore a rawhide thong around his neck, tightened there by his captors. Then they set out. So long as he didn't fall down, the Crows ignored him. On the second day, one of the Indians threw him a pair of moccasins.

He thought constantly of escape, hoping to be killed in flight rather than this slow torture, but he had no chance to try. The Crow were more familiar with escape than he. Knowing what to expect, they forestalled it. The only other time he had attempted an escape was in Boston from his family, and he had succeeded. Then, his father had raged and his grandmother had cried, but they could not stop him from leaving.

Before riding into camp, the Crow Indians dressed in their regalia. They also wore articles of their victims' clothing. They painted their faces black. Then leading the white man by the rawhide thong, they rode down toward the tepee circle, shouting and singing, brandishing their weapons. When he fell, they did not stop but dragged him into camp.

Dazed and battered, he lay where they had left him in front of a tepee. The noisy, busy life of the camp swarmed around him, and people came to stare. Thirst consumed him. When it rained, he lapped water from the ground like a dog. A scrawny, shrieking old woman with graying hair threw a chunk of meat on the grass, and he fought the dogs for it.

When his head cleared, he was angry, although anger was an emotion he knew he could not afford. The hag now gave him stinking, rancid grease and let him figure out what to do with it. He applied it gingerly to his sun-seared body.

While he was healing, he considered coldly the advantages of being a horse, for that was how his captors had treated him. A man who was humiliated would strike back sooner or later, and that would be the end of him. A horse, however, had only to be docile. Very well, he would do without his pride. He understood now that he belonged to the screaming old woman, a gift from her son that she liked to show off.

The white man, who now thought of himself as a horse, forgot sometimes to worry about his danger. He kept making mental notes of things to tell his people in Boston about this hideous adventure. He would go back a hero, and he would say, "Grandmother, let me fetch your shawl. I'm accustomed to doing errands for a lady about your age."

Two girls lived in the tepee with the old hag and her warrior son. One, the white man concluded, was his captor's wife and the other his younger sister. The daughter-in-law was smug and spoiled. Being beloved, she did not have to be useful. The sister had bright eyes that often wandered to the man who was pretending to be a horse.

The two girls worked when the old woman put them at it, but they often ran off to do something they enjoyed more. There were games, noisy contests, and much laughter throughout the camp. The white man was finding out what loneliness could be.

The captive was a horse all summer, a docile bearer of burdens. He kept reminding himself that he had to be better-natured than horses because he could not lash out with hooves or teeth. Even among horses he felt unequal. If they escaped, they could fend for themselves, but he would simply starve. Humbly, he fetched and carried. When the camp moved, he carried pack, trudging with the women. Even the dogs worked then, pulling sledges made of sticks.

The Indian who had captured him lived like a lord, as was his right. He hunted, attended meetings with much chanting and dancing, and lounged in the shade with his smug bride. He had two responsibilities—to kill buffalo and to gain glory.

One day in early fall several things happened that made the captive think he might in time become a man again. This was the day when he began to understand their language.

When the young women set out for the river, one of them called over her shoulder to the old woman. The white man was startled. She had said she was going to bathe. His understanding was so sudden that he felt as if his ears had come unstopped.

On the same day the old woman brought a pair of new moccasins out of the tepee and tossed them on the ground before him. In thanking her, Horse dared greatly. He picked a handful of flowers and took them to her as she squatted in front of her tepee, scraping a buffalo hide. Her hands were hideous—most of her fingers had the first joints missing. He bowed and offered the flowers.

She glared up at him from the ragged tangle of her hair. Then she knocked the flowers out of his hand and ran to the next tepee, telling the story. The other women screamed with laughter.

The white man squared his shoulders and walked boldly over to watch three small boys shooting arrows at a target. He said in English, "Show me how to do that, will you?" They frowned, but he held out his hand as if in no doubt. One of them gave him a bow and one arrow, and they snickered when he missed.

A few days later, he asked the hag, with gestures, for a bow that her son had just discarded, a man-size bow made of horn. Each day, he scavenged for arrows. The old woman and her neighbors cackled at his marksmanship. In time, his aim improved.

Now that he understood words, he identified the Crow by their names. The old woman was Greasy Hand, and her daughter was Pretty Calf. The man who had captured him was Yellow Robe.

He began to talk a little and was less lonely. He asked the old woman, "What is my name?" Until he knew it, he was incomplete. She shrugged to let him know he had none. He told her in the Crow language "My name is Horse." He repeated it, and she nodded. After that they called him Horse when they called him anything. Nobody cared except the white man himself.

They trusted him enough to let him stray out of camp. He might have run away, but winter was too close. He did not dare leave without a horse, clothing, and a better weapon for hunting. On a cold night he crept inside the tepee after the others had gone to bed. Even a horse might try to find shelter from the wind. The old woman grumbled, but she did not put him out. They tolerated him, back in the shadows, so long as he did not get in the way.

He began to understand how the family that owned him differed from the others. Fate had been cruel to them. One old woman derided Greasy Hand by sneering, "You have no relatives!" and Greasy Hand raved for minutes of the deeds of her father, uncles, brothers, and four sons. Her detractor answered with scorn, "Where are they now?"

Later the white man found her moaning and whimpering, rocking back and forth and staring at her mutilated hands. By that time, he understood. A mourner often chopped off a finger joint. Old Greasy Hand had mourned often. He felt a twinge of pity, but put it aside as another emotion that he could not afford. He thought: *What tales I will tell when I get home!*

He did not trust the old woman. Just how fitful her temper was he saw one day when she got tired of stumbling over a large dog that pulled baggage when the tribe moved camp. Countless times he had seen her kick at the beast as it slept in front of the tepee. One day, she gave the dog its usual kick and stood scolding while the animal rolled its eyes sleepily. Then she suddenly picked up her ax and cut off the dog's head. Looking well-satisfied, she beckoned her slave to remove the body.

It could have been me, he thought, if I were a dog. But I am a horse.

His hope of life lay with the girl, Pretty Calf. The custom of courtship required a gift of horses to a girl's older brother and of buffalo meat to her mother. He owned no horse and no weapon but the old bow and battered arrows. Back home he could have married any girl he wished, but he wasted little time thinking of that. Among the Crow, a future was something to be earned.

The most he dared do was wink at Pretty Calf or speak admiringly of her. At those times, she giggled and hid her face. The least he dared do was to elope, but first he had to give her a horse to put the seal of tribal approval on that. His chance came in early spring when he was hunting small game with three young boys, his guards and scornful companions. After walking far, they saw two horses in a sheltered ravine. The boys and the man crawled forward and saw an Indian moaning on the ground, a lone traveler. From the way the boys eagerly inched forward, Horse knew the man was an enemy and fair prey.

The white man shot an arrow into the sick man, a split second ahead of the boys. Dashing forward, he struck the still-groaning man with his bow, to count a first blow, and seized the hobbled horses. By the time he had the horses, one of the boys had the Indian's scalp.

That evening they rode into camp, two of them on each horse. Indians who had ignored him as a slave stared at the brave man who had struck a first blow and had stolen horses. The excitement lasted all night. The white man had watched warriors in their triumph and knew what to do. When a man did something big, he told about it. The white man smeared his face with grease and charcoal and walked inside the tepee circle, chanting and singing.

"You heathens, you savages," he chanted in English. "I'm going to get out of here someday! I'm going to get away!" The Crow people listened respectfully. In the Crow tongue he shouted, "Horse! I am Horse!" and they nodded. He had a right to boast. He owned two horses. He looked at Pretty Calf. Now he would have a wife.

Before dawn the white man and his bride were sheltered beyond a far hill, and he was telling her, "I love you, little lady, I love you." She looked at him with the great dark eyes and seemed to understand. "You are my treasure," he said, "more precious than jewels, better than fine gold. I am going to call you Freedom."

When they returned to camp two days later, Old Greasy Hand raged—but not at him. She complained that her daughter had let herself go too cheap, but the marriage was as good as any. He had paid a horse.

He learned the language faster after that because of the attentions of his adoring wife. Pretty Calf delighted in educating him. She giggled when she told him, in his ignorance, of things she had always known. Greasy Hand no longer spoke to him, for there could be no conversation between a man and his mother-in-law. He was no longer a horse, but a kind of man—a half-Indian living on the fringes of Crow society.

He did not plan on how he would get home. Instead, he dreamed of being there all at once and telling stories no one would believe. There was no hurry.

One day, Yellow Robe's wife was taken by another warrior. Yellow Robe belonged to a society called the Big Dogs. The wife stealer, Cut Neck, belonged to the Foxes. They were fellow tribesmen, but men of one society could take away wives from the other under certain conditions. When Cut Neck rode up to the tepee, laughing and singing, and called to Yellow Robe's wife, "Come out! Come out!" she did as ordered, looking smug and willing. Thereafter she rode beside him in ceremonial processions, while his other wife pretended not to care.

"But why?" the white man demanded of his wife, his Freedom. "Why did your brother let her go? He sits and does not speak."

Pretty Calf explained that her brother's wife could have hidden from Cut Neck or have refused to go. Her brother could not possibly let her come back—or admit that his heart was sick. That would be dishonor.

There was no sense in it. The white man glared at his young wife. "If you go, I will bring you back."

"I will not go," she promised, and then murmured "*Hayha.*" When he did not answer, she said, "A woman calls her man that if she thinks he will not leave her. Am I wrong?"

The white man held her closer and lied. "Pretty Calf is not wrong. Horse will not leave her." What he was thinking was this: *Parting from this one was going to be harder than getting her had been.* "Hayha," he whispered. "Freedom."

His conscience irked him, but not very much. Pretty Calf could get another man easily enough when he was gone, a better provider. There was no hurry about leaving, though. He owned five horses now and was secure.

The grass grew yellow on the plains, and the long cold was close. He was enslaved by the girl he called Freedom, and before winter ended by the knowledge they would have a child.

In the spring the Big Dog society held a long ceremony. The white man was not a part of it, and he strolled with his woman along the creek bank, thinking: *When I get home I will tell them about the chants and the drumming. Sometime. . . .*

Inside the tepee, Pretty Calf would not go to bed. "I must know about my brother," she urged. "Something may happen." Even the old woman, who was a great one for getting sleep when she was not working, prowled around restlessly. When Yellow Robe returned at last in his paint and feathers, the women cried out, but the conversation was too fast for Horse to follow. When the white man went to sleep, he thought his wife was weeping.

The next morning she explained. "He wears the bearskin belt. Now he can never retreat in battle. He will die."

She recalled that a few men honored by the bearskin belt had lived through the summer and were free of it. "But my brother wants to die," she mourned. "His heart is bitter."

Yellow Robe lived through half a dozen clashes with raiders from hostile tribes. His honors were many. He captured horses in an enemy camp and led two successful raids. He spent much time in prayer alone in the hills, or in conference with a medicine man. But before he could be free of the honor of the bearskin belt, he went on his last raid. The Crow warriors put his body in a cave and walled it in with rocks.

There was blood on the ground before the tepee to which Yellow Robe would return no more. His mother with her hair chopped short sat within the doorway, rocking back and forth on her haunches, wailing her heartbreak. She cradled one mutilated hand in the other. She had cut off another finger joint.

Pretty Calf was crying as she gashed her arms with a knife. The white man tried to take the knife away, but she protested so piteously that he let her do as she wished. He was sickened with the lot of them. *Savages,* he thought.

Now I will go back! I'll hunt alone and keep moving. . . . Still, he did not go just yet. He was the only hunter in the lodge of the two grieving women.

In their mourning, they made him a pauper again. Everything was sacrificed to the spirits because of the death of Yellow Robe. The tepee made of buffalo hides, the furs that should have kept them warm, the white deer-skin dress that Pretty Calf loved so well, even their tools and Yellow Robe's weapons, they left on the prairie, and the whole camp moved away. Two of his best horses were killed as a sacrifice, and the women gave away the meat.

Yellow Robe's women had no relatives with whom they might have lived. For two months of mourning, they would have no tepee. Their shelter was a temporary hut of willows. Horse was furious at their foolishness. It had been bad enough for him to be a captive and a slave. Now these women had voluntarily given up everything he had worked hard to attain.

Too angry to sleep in the willow hut, he lay under a sheltering tree. On the third night of mourning, he made his plans. He had a knife and a bow. He would go after meat, taking two horses, and not come back. There was much, he realized, he was not going to tell when he got home. In the willow hut, Pretty Calf cried out. He heard rustling there, and the woman's querulous voice.

Some twenty hours later his son was born, two months early. The child was born without breath, and the mother died before the sun went down.

The white man was too shocked to think whether he should mourn, or even how he should mourn. The old woman screamed until she was voiceless. Piteously, she approached him, bent and trembling, blind with grief. She held out her knife, and he took it. She spread out her hands and shook her head. If she cut off any more finger joints, she could not work.

The white man said, "All right! All right!" between his teeth. He hacked his arms with the knife and stood watching his blood run. It was little enough to do for Pretty Calf, for Freedom.

He looked at Greasy Hand, hideous in her grief-burdened age, and thought: *I really am free now! When a wife dies, her husband has no more duty toward her family.* Pretty Calf had told him so, long ago.

The old woman, of course, would be a scavenger. One other ancient crone of the tribe had no relatives. She lived on food thrown away by the more fortunate. She slept in shelters built with her own knotted hands. When the camp moved, she followed wearily alone.

Tomorrow morning, the white man decided, *I will go.*

His mother-in-law's sunken mouth quivered. She said one word questioningly. She said, "*Eero-oshay?* Son?"

Blinking, he remembered. When a wife died, her husband was free. But her mother, who had ignored him with dignity, might if she wished ask him to stay. Now Greasy Hand invited him to do so by calling him Son.

She stood before him, bowed with years of labor, scarred with grief. But with all her burdens, she still loved life enough to beg it from him, the only person she had any right to ask. She was stripping herself of all she had left—her pride.

He looked eastward across the prairie. Two thousand miles away was home. The old woman would not live forever. He could afford to wait, for he was young. He could be magnanimous, for now he knew he was a man and not a horse.

"*Eegya,*" he said. "Mother."

He went home three years later. He explained only, "I lived with the Crows for a while. It was some time before I could leave. They called me Horse."

He found it unnecessary either to apologize for having run away or to boast for having returned. He did not think of himself as a hero. But his discontent was gone. He was the equal of any man on Earth.

The Country of the Blind

by H. G. Wells

IN THE VALLEY OF THE BLIND, THE ONE-EYED MAN IS KING. OR SO NUÑEZ BELIEVED. LITTLE DID HE KNOW THAT HIS SIGHT MADE HIM AN OUTCAST.

*T*hree hundred miles and more from Chimborzo, one hundred from the snows of Cotopaxi, in the wildest wastes of Ecuador's Andes, where the frost-and-sun-rotted rocks rise in vast pinnacles and cliffs above the snows, there was once a mysterious mountain valley called the Country of the Blind. Long years ago, or so legend says, people from a small village fled their evil Spanish ruler. They packed everything they owned on the backs of llamas and crossed these steep mountains peaks. For days they clambered through frightful gorges and over an icy pass into at last a valley of sweet-tasting water, green meadows, and rich soil. Soon after came a stupendous storm. One whole side of the mountain crest avalanched, slid down in thunder, and cut off this Country of the Blind forever.

One settler had been on the opposite side of the avalanche when the world had so terribly shaken itself. He could not return, even though he had a wife and a child among the settlers in the valley. He started his life over again in the South American town of Quito, but he kept the legend of the Country of the Blind alive. He told anyone who would listen—and many did, though just as many scoffed at his stories—of the mysterious valley. A circle of ice-capped precipices of gray-green rock brooded over that glowing garden, but only rarely did snow reach the valley. The settlers had prospered, the man said.

Only one thing spoiled their happiness. Some sinister quality hid in that sweet and bracing air, or perhaps in the glacier lake's ancient water. A strange disease had come upon the people so that all the children born to them were blind. Their eyes shrank away to nothing until only empty sockets remained in their faces. In time, the people forgot what seeing was.

A mountaineer from Bogotá, Colombia, a man who had been down to the sea and had seen the world, did not believe the story. His name was Nuñez. He had agreed to join a small climbing party of Englishmen to replace a guide who had fallen ill. One night while camped on an icy rock ledge high in the mountains, the group of climbers retold the story of the Country of the Blind. "There is no truth to it," swore Nuñez. "And yet, if it were true and we were to stumble into this meadow, then we should become its rulers."

"How so?" asked one of the Englishmen.

"There is an old proverb," Nuñez said. "In the country of the blind, even the one-eyed man is king!" With that, Nuñez ducked out of his companions' tent. The wind swallowed his laughter as he stepped toward his own tent, barely visible in the blowing snow.

By morning, the wind had subsided. The English climbers emerged from their snow-laden tents and discovered that Nuñez had disappeared. They shouted and whistled, but there was no reply. They made a cramped search for him and found the traces of his fall. The depths had snatched him down. He had slipped eastward toward the unknown side of the mountain. Far below, he had struck a steep slope of snow, and ploughed his way down. His track went straight to the edge of a precipice. Beyond that, everything was hidden.

Far, far below, and hazy with the distance, they could see trees rising out of a narrow, shut-in valley. They did not know it was the lost Country of the Blind, for it looked no different from any other narrow streak of sheltered upland valley.

One of the Englishmen spoke up. "Someone must at least attempt to rescue him."

The surviving guide shook his head. "No one could survive that fall. We cannot risk our own lives for one that has already been lost."

And so, reluctantly, the mountain climbing party left Nuñez to his fate.

This man who fell survived.

He fell a thousand feet, and came down in the midst of a cloud of snow upon a snow slope even steeper than the one above. Down this he was again whirled, stunned and insensible. At last, he rolled out and lay still, buried amidst a softening heap of the white masses that had accompanied him and—miraculously—saved him.

When he woke, he thought dimly that he was ill in bed. And then he saw the stars, and he remembered falling, falling through wind and snow and darkness, falling like a bird without wings. He lay flat upon his chest for a space, wondering where he was. He explored his limbs. They ached exceedingly, but they were unbroken.

He looked up to see, exaggerated by the ghastly light of the rising moon, the tremendous flight he had taken. For a while he lay, gazing blankly at that vast pale cliff towering above, rising moment by moment out of a subsiding tide of darkness. Dawn was breaking beyond the points of the distant peaks. Soon birds began to sing. Nuñez sat up stiffly and turned eastward. Between walls of jagged rock was a gorge full of snow and sunshine. He followed it until it came to a narrow, sheer waterfall of melting snow and ice. Beyond was a valley of green meadows. Flocks of some kind of animal grazed. Beyond the meadow were the rooftops of small houses. A desperate man might venture down the waterfall's face and survive. Nuñez looked behind him at the top of the world from where he had come without food and climbing gear.

At midday he emerged from the shadow of the falls into the sunlight again. He was now only a few hundred yards from the valley meadows. He now saw that the grazing animals were llamas. He spied also a number of men and women resting on piled heaps of grass, as if taking a siesta. Nearer to him a line of three men carried pails on yokes along a little path that ran from the encircling wall toward the houses. The men were clad in garments of llama cloth and boots and belts of leather, and they wore caps of cloth with back and ear flaps.

Nuñez shouted. A thousand echoes rang round and round the valley.

The three men stopped and moved their heads as if they were looking about them. They turned their faces this way and that. Nuñez waved his arms, but they did not appear to see him. Nuñez bawled again and then once more he waved. He crossed the stream by a little bridge and approached them. They turned their ears, not their eyes, toward the sounds of his footsteps. At once, Nuñez stopped.

They were blind. Could the legend really be true? Had he found the lost Country of the Blind?

"A man," one said, in hardly recognizable Spanish—"a man it is—a man or a beast that walks like a man—coming down from the rocks."

Nuñez stepped forward with confidence. All the old stories of the lost valley came back to his mind and especially the proverb *In the Country of the Blind the One-Eyed Man Is King.*

"I came from over the mountains," Nuñez announced. "I came from a land where men can see."

"He comes," said the second blind man, "from out of the rocks."

They startled him by a sudden movement toward him, each with a hand outstretched. Nuñez stepped back from the advance of these spread fingers.

"Come hither," said the blind man, following Nuñez's motion and clutching him neatly.

They held Nuñez and felt him over, saying no further word until they had done so.

"Carefully," he cried, when a finger was poked in his eyes, and he realized that they thought that organ, with its fluttering lids, a queer thing in him. They felt over it again.

"A strange creature, Correa," said the one called Pedro. "Feel the coarseness of his hair. Like a llama's hair."

"Rough he is as the rocks that gave him birth," said Correa, investigating Nuñez's unshaven chin with a soft and slightly moist hand.

"Careful!" Nuñez cried again.

"He speaks," said the third man. "Certainly he is a man."

"Let us lead him to the elders," said Pedro.

"Shout first," said Correa, "lest the children be afraid. This is a marvelous occasion."

So they shouted, and Pedro went first and took Nuñez by the hand to lead him to the houses.

Nuñez drew his hand away. "I can see," he said.

"See?" said Correa.

"Yes, see," said Nuñez, turning toward, and stumbled against Pedro's pail.

"His senses are still imperfect," said the third blind man. "He stumbles, and talks unmeaning words. Lead him by the hand."

"As you will," said Nuñez, smiling. He had much he would teach these people. He would rule them. He would be king.

The village seemed larger as he drew near to it. The houses stood in a continuous row on either side of a central street of astonishing cleanness; here and there in the plaster smeared walls of the houses were doors but not a single window. The villagers mobbed him, holding on to him, touching him with soft, sensitive hands, smelling at him, and listening for every word he spoke. Some of the maidens and children, however, kept aloof as if afraid, and indeed his voice sounded rude and coarse in comparison to their sweeter, softer notes.

"Bogotá!" Nuñez struck his chest. "Bogotá. Over the mountain crests."

"A wild man—using wild words," said Pedro. "His mind is hardly formed yet. He has only the beginnings of speech."

A brave little boy nipped his head. "Bogotá!" he said mockingly.

"It is a city to your village. I come from a great world—where men have eyes and see."

"His name's Bogotá!" they said.

They thrust him through a doorway into a room as black as pitch, save at the end there faintly glowed a fire. The crowd closed in behind him and shut out all but the faintest glimmer of day. Before he could allow his eyes to adjust to the darkness, he fell headlong over the feet of a seated man. His arm, outflung, struck the face of someone else as he went down. He felt the soft impact of features and heard a cry of anger. "I can't see in this darkness," he said, angry now himself. He struggled against a number of hands that clutched him. It was a one-sided fight. An inkling of the situation came to him, and he lay quiet.

"May I sit up?" he asked. "I will not struggle against you again."

They let him rise.

The voice of an older man began to question him, and Nuñez found himself trying to explain the great world out of which he had fallen—the sky, the mountains. The elders who sat in darkness in the Country of the Blind believed not a word.

"I told you, Yacob," warned Pedro. "He is evil. Feel the lumps on his face."

"No, he is not evil. He came from the rocks to serve us. In time, Bogotá will learn our ways."

"Serve you!" Nuñez repeated incredulously as the blind men led him away.

Left alone, Nuñez muttered to himself, "An unformed mind! No senses yet! They little know they've been mistreating their heaven-sent master. I see I must bring them to reason. But how? Let me think—let me think."

He was still thinking when a young woman came to him with llama's milk in a bowl and rough salted bread. Nuñez stared at her. She was not like the others. Her eye sockets were smooth circles, not black and sunken holes like those of the others in the village. She had long eyelashes, something the others seemed not to have.

"Your face," said Nuñez. "It is beautiful."

"I am ugly," she said softly. "The others say so. The children tease me about the hairy lashes that grow on my face."

"They don't see your beauty as I do," he said. "Your skin is white as snow."

"What is white?"

"A color." He lightly touched her cheek.

Quickly, she drew away. "Do not speak of things you do not understand. Yacob is my father and he will kill you if you do not learn our ways." And then she slipped away.

Throughout the remainder of the afternoon, the village slept. Nuñez slumbered not at all. It seemed to him that the glow upon the distant snowfields and glaciers that rose about the valley on every side was the most beautiful sight he had ever seen. His eyes went from that glory to the village and irrigated fields, fast sinking into the twilight. Suddenly, a wave of emotion shook him. He thanked God from the bottom of his heart that He had given him the gift of sight.

He heard a voice calling. "Bogotá! Come here!"

Nuñez stood up, smiling. Now he would show these people once and for all what sight could do for a man. He laughed noiselessly and stepped stealthily from the stone path, hiding in the shadows.

"Trample not the grass, Bogotá. That is not allowed."

Nuñez had scarcely heard the sound he made himself. He stopped, amazed.

"Why did you not come when I called you?" asked Yacob. "Must you be led like a child? Can you not hear the path as you walk?"

"I can *see* the path."

"There is no such thing as *see*. Cease this folly and follow the sound of my feet."

Nuñez followed, annoyed.

Four days passed. The fifth day found the King of the Blind still a clumsy, useless stranger among his subjects. He discovered that it was going to be more difficult to proclaim himself master than he had supposed. First, he had tried persuasion. He spoke of the beauties of sight, of a sky full of stars and clouds and an orb called "moon" that changed shapes. They answered by saying there were no mountains, only rocks. A great roof covered the world and the world was only this place. As for the great warmth during the nighttime, that was the power of Wisdom Above.

Next, he argued. Light was day. Dark was night. People worked in light. People slept in dark. He saw also that Yacob's youngest daughter Medina *was* listening, though she did not speak.

At last, he rebelled. While working in the field, he seized his spade and swung it above his head. The others heard the faint sound through the air and turned, suddenly alert to danger as an animal might be.

"I am king of the blind!" he shouted. "I am the one-eyed king!"

"He is crazier now than when we first found him," said Pedro.

Nuñez was determined to prove the value of sight, in combat if necessary. He gripped the spade, ready to bring it down upon Pedro's hooded skull. Then he discovered something new about himself. He could not strike a blind man in cold blood.

"Put that spade down," said one man.

Nuñez felt a helpless horror. *How* could they know?

The blind men circled him silently.

"Stay away! I will hurt you! I will!" Nuñez threatened. They closed upon him.

Nuñez struck Pedro across the back, dropped the spade, and then charged through the circle. He ran and ran, away from the meadow and the windowless houses. He fled, leaving a track of trampled grass. And then he sat and rested and wondered what he should do now.

Then he saw them. They came stooping and feeling their way along the trampled grass. Some sniffed. Others stood still and listened.

His pulse rang in his ears. He looked behind him at the sheer wall of rocks, impossible to climb without ropes and chisels and spikes. Then he looked again at his pursuers. They were groping, but moving rapidly toward him.

"You don't understand!" Nuñez suddenly cried out. "You are blind and I can see. Leave me alone!" He ran again.

For two nights he stayed outside the wall of the Valley of the Blind. For two nights and days he had no shelter from the cold mountain air. He had no weapons. He scavenged for food from the shrublike bushes, but the leaves made his stomach cramp and retch. His hunger and sickness weakened him. Finally, he crawled down to the wall of the village. They seized him at once and took him to Yacob.

"I was mad," Nuñez said. "But I was only newly made. I did not know what I was doing."

"Do you still believe you can see?" asked Yacob.

Nuñez's stomach was a knot of hunger. "No."

"Do you still believe there is a world beyond this place?"

Nuñez began to weep. "I am hungry. Give me food. Please."

"What is overhead?" asked Yacob. "Stars? Clouds?"

"About ten times the height of man there is a roof above the world . . . made of rock and very smooth," Nuñez answered. "Please, I am not well."

Yacob regarded Nuñez's rebellion as further evidence of his inferiority. He had not killed Pedro as Nuñez had first feared. His punishment was a public whipping and then confinement to a dark place with only a locked door. The darkness was misery for Nuñez.

Medina nursed him. She unlocked the door and entered with food. At first, they did not speak. Then courage returned to Nuñez when one evening Medina shyly asked, "Bogotá, what is color?"

"I can't describe it!" he said, frustrated. "I wish you could see what I see—sunlight like diamonds on the snow, leaves dancing on the trees in the wind."

"We feel the wind, Bogotá. It's cool and sometimes smells of pine. But," she chided him softly, "no one *sees* it."

He risked never being set free of the dark hut by insisting, "But I do. *I* see it."

In time, Yacob set him free and appointed him to do the simplest, heaviest work in the village. This Nuñez did, for at least it meant that he could be near Medina. One evening he went to where she was sitting in the summer moonlight spinning. The light made her a thing of silver and mystery. He sat down at her feet and told her he loved her. Medina, with her long thick eyelashes, was considered a disfigured woman in the Country of the Blind. She had never heard words of adoration or love.

From the first there was great opposition to the marriage of Nuñez and Medina, not because the village valued her but rather because they thought Nuñez an idiot, an incompetent thing below the level of a man. Old Yacob, however, had a tenderness for his last little daughter, deformed as she was, and he grieved when she moaned upon his shoulder. "He is better than he was, Father. He's strong and kind," Medina pleaded. "He loves me and I love him."

Yacob had grown fond of Bogotá, as well, though he still considered him stupid. But marriage was impossible unless . . .

"I have examined Bogotá," said one of the elders, a great doctor. "I think he might be cured. Those growths on his face that he calls eyes have diseased his brain. Skin and a fringe of hair cover the lumps. The lumps themselves move and are quite tender to the touch."

"Yes?" Yacob asked.

"In order to cure him completely all that we need do is a simple and easy surgical operation—namely to remove those irritating growths."

"And then he will be sane?"

"Perfectly sane."

Yacob went to Nuñez and told him of the doctor's proposal.

"You want me to lose my gift of sight?" Nuñez asked.

"If you love my daughter, you must do this. Then I shall agree to the marriage."

Medina persuaded Nuñez to face the blind surgeon. Nuñez could not believe Medina would wish such a thing. "My world is sight," he told her.

"Your world is imagination," she said.

"If only to look upon you and your serene face, I must keep my sight!"

"I wish," she said, "sometimes . . ." She paused. "I wish sometimes you would not talk like that. I love hearing about stars and flowers and colors, but . . . perhaps father is right. You would not be so angry and so unhappy if you let the surgeon do his work."

He felt anger, indeed anger at the dull course of fate, but also sympathy for her lack of understanding. He pitied her. He put his arms around her and they sat quietly for a long time. Then he asked, "If I consent to this . . ."

She flung her arms around him. "Oh, if only you would."

"Are you certain you want me to do this?"

"It would hurt you but little and you would be going through this pain for me and I will repay you. I will repay you for the rest of my life!"

"So be it," he said.

could not see Medina any longer, and he could not see the shifting cliffs because of their blows and because of the blood that poured from the cuts on his forehead. They thrust him through the opening in the village wall. "There you stay and starve!" said one. "You and your—*seeing.*" They blocked the entrance to the village.

Nuñez stood swaying like a drunken man. Then the ground stopped rolling, and the world was silent once more. But for how long? Nuñez wiped the blood from his eyes and squinted through his pain at the mountain to the east. The rockfall had exposed a chimney up which he could climb, climb into the snows and from there to Bogotá. He could escape.

"What is the good of going alone?" he said to himself. "Even if I could, I shall only starve up there."

And then he saw Medina. She had slipped through the barrier in the village wall, seeking him. "Bogotá, my darling," she cried. "What have they done to you? Oh, *what* have they *done* to you?

He staggered to meet her.

"Why did you behave so madly?" she cried. "If you come back now, they will surely kill you. But I will bring you food."

The earth shuddered again. This shock wave was stronger than the first. "Neither of us can stay here now. Come, do not question, just come!"

He drew her to him with a renewal of strength. If they could reach that distant rock shelf, they might yet survive. "Climb!" he ordered. "Climb!"

"I do not understand."

She had never been to the rocks, to the mountain. She had never climbed. He guided her feet and her hands, smearing her with his blood. A rush of terrified llamas crowded past them.

"What is happening? Why are these creatures here?"

"Because they know the valley is doomed. Climb."

They reached the shelf and flattened themselves against the rock. Below, Nuñez saw the ground split open. For a tense moment, the world seemed to hang suspended, and the mountain in the west collapsed upon itself and the valley below. A stunning concussion struck his chest a giant's blow. Medina clung to the rock shelf with clawing hands. Mud and broken rock fragments pelted them. The wave of debris surged and receded and abruptly became still. Then colossal pillars of dust rose up solemnly and unfolded and rolled about them like a stinging fog.

Nuñez opened his eyes. For once he was grateful that Medina could not see, for the Country of the Blind was no more.

Two days later, a hunting party that had come to the mountains to explore the scene of the disaster found them in the snow. They had lived upon water, fern roots, and a few berries. They did not believe their story. The Country of the Blind did not exist, they said.

Nuñez brought Medina to his people in Bogotá. She was a sweet and gentle wife and in time, she became a sweet and gentle mother. Her child was as stout and sturdy as his father. He had his father's eyes, as well. Medina loved her son, but she was not able to protect him as she had once protected Nuñez. In this world of sight, much of the comings and goings about her were difficult to understand. She rarely spoke of the Country of the Blind or of her childhood there, being painfully teased by the others for the hairy lashes upon her face. And yet, she was lonelier here in Bogotá.

One day, her oldest child dared to ask why his mother did not go to a surgeon so that she might be able to see and be like all the other people. The boy had no way of knowing, of course, that Medina had once made this same request of Nuñez. "Don't you want to look at me? Don't you love me?" the little boy asked.

"I don't need to *see* you to know what you are like or that I love you."

"But haven't you ever wanted to see, Mama?"

"No. Never."

"But colors . . ." the child began, "and stars and all the beautiful things . . ."

"They may be beautiful," said Medina, "but it must be very terrible to *see*."

PART III
The Rebels

Charles

by Shirley Jackson

*CHARLES WAS BAD—SO BAD THEY MIGHT
JUST THROW HIM OUT OF SCHOOL.*

*T*he day my son Laurie started kindergarten he renounced corduroy overalls with bibs and began wearing blue jeans with a belt. I watched him go off the first morning with the older girl next door, seeing clearly that an era of my life was ended, my sweet-voiced nursery-school tot replaced by a long-trousered, swaggering character who forgot to stop at the corner and wave good-bye.

He came home the same way, the front door slamming open, his cap on the floor, and the voice suddenly raucous, shouting "Isn't anybody *here*?"

At lunch he spoke insolently to his father, spilled his baby sister's milk, and remarked that his teacher said that we were not to take the name of the Lord in vain.

"How *was* school today?" I asked, elaborately casual.

"All right," he said.

"Did you learn anything?" his father asked.

Laurie regarded his father coldly. "I didn't learn nothing," he said.

"Anything," I said. "Didn't learn anything."

"The teacher spanked a boy, though," Laurie said, addressing his bread and butter. "For being fresh," he added, with his mouth full.

"What did he do?" I asked. "Who was it?"

Laurie thought. "It was Charles," he said. "He was fresh. The teacher spanked him and made him stand in a corner. He was awfully fresh."

"What did he do?" I asked again, but Laurie slid off his chair, took a cookie, and left, while his father was still saying "See here, young man."

The next day Laurie remarked at lunch, as soon as he sat down, "Well, Charles was bad again today." He grinned enormously and said, "Today Charles hit the teacher."

"Good heavens," I said, mindful of the Lord's name. "I suppose he got spanked again?"

"He sure did," Laurie said. "Look up," he said to his father.

"What?" his father said, looking up.

"Look down," Laurie said. "Look at my thumb. Gee, you're dumb." He began to laugh insanely.

"Why did Charles hit the teacher?" I asked quickly.

"Because she tried to make him color with red crayons," Laurie said. "Charles wanted to color with green crayons, so he hit the teacher and she spanked him and said nobody should play with Charles but everybody did."

The third day—it was Wednesday of the first week—Charles bounced a seesaw onto the head of a little girl and made her bleed, and the teacher made him stay inside all during recess. Thursday, Charles had to stand in a corner during storytime because he kept pounding his feet on the floor. Friday, Charles was deprived of blackboard privileges because he threw chalk.

On Saturday I remarked to my husband, "Do you think kindergarten is too unsettling for Laurie? All this toughness, and bad grammar, and this Charles boy sounds like such a bad influence."

"It'll be all right," my husband said reassuringly. "Bound to be people like Charles in the world. Might as well meet them now as later."

On Monday, Laurie came home late, full of news. "Charles," he shouted as he came up the hill. I was waiting anxiously on the front steps. "Charles," Laurie yelled all the way up the hill, "Charles was bad again."

"Come right in," I said, as soon as he came close enough. "Lunch is waiting."

"You know what Charles did?" he demanded, following me through the door. "Charles yelled so in school they sent a boy in from the first grade to tell the teacher she had to make Charles keep quiet, and so Charles had to stay after school. And so all the children stayed to watch him."

"What did he do?" I asked.

"He just sat there," Laurie said, climbing into his chair at the table. "Hi, Pop, y'old dust mop."

"Charles had to stay after school today," I told my husband. "Everyone stayed with him."

"What does Charles look like?" my husband asked Laurie. "What's his other name?"

"He's bigger than me," Laurie said. "And he doesn't ever wear a jacket."

Monday night was the first Parent-Teacher meeting, and only the fact that the baby had a cold kept me from going; I wanted passionately to meet Charles's mother. On Tuesday, Laurie remarked suddenly, "Our teacher had a friend come to see her in school today."

"Charles's mother?" my husband and I asked simultaneously.

"Naah," Laurie said scornfully. "It was a man who came and made us do exercises; we had to touch our toes. Look." He climbed down from this chair and squatted down. "Like this," he said. He got solemnly back into his chair and said, picking up his fork, "Charles didn't even do exercises."

"That's fine," I said heartily. "Didn't Charles want to do exercises?"

"Naah," Laurie said. "Charles was so fresh to the teacher's friend he wasn't *let* do exercises."

"Fresh again?" I said.

"He kicked the teacher's friend," Laurie said. "The teacher's friend told Charles to touch his toes like I just did, and Charles kicked him."

"What are they going to do about Charles, do you suppose?" Laurie's father asked.

Laurie shrugged elaborately. "Throw him out of school, I guess," he said.

Wednesday and Thursday were routine; Charles yelled during story hour and hit a boy in the stomach and made him cry. On Friday, Charles stayed after school and so did all the other children.

With the third week of kindergarten Charles was an institution in our family; the baby was being a Charles when she cried all afternoon; Laurie did a Charles when he filled his wagon full of mud and pulled it through the kitchen; even my husband, when he caught his elbow in the telephone cord and pulled the telephone, ashtray, and a bowl of flowers off the table, said "Looks like Charles."

During the third and fourth weeks it looked like a reformation in Charles. Laurie reported grimly at lunch on Thursday of the third week, "Charles was so good today the teacher gave him an apple."

"What?" I said, and my husband added warily, "You mean Charles?"

"Charles," Laurie said. "He gave the crayons around and he picked up the books afterward and the teacher said he was her helper."

"What happened?" I asked incredulously.

"He was her helper, that's all," Laurie said, and shrugged.

"Can this be true?" I asked my husband that night. "Can something like this happen?"

"Wait and see," my husband said cynically. "When you've got a Charles to deal with, this may mean he's only plotting."

He seemed to be wrong. For over a week Charles was the teacher's helper. Each day he handed things out and he picked things up. No one had to stay after school.

"The P.T.A. meeting's next week again," I told my husband one evening. "I'm going to find Charles's mother there."

"Ask her what happened to Charles," my husband said. "I'd like to know."

"I'd like to know myself," I said.

On Friday of that week things were back to normal. "You know what Charles did today?" Laurie demanded at the lunch table, in a voice slightly awed. "He told a little girl to say a word and she said it and the teacher washed her mouth out with soap and Charles laughed."

"What word?" his father asked quite unwisely, and Laurie said, "I'll have to whisper it to you, it's so bad." He got down off his chair and went around to his father. His father bent his head down and Laurie whispered joyfully. His father's eyes widened.

"Did Charles tell the little girl to say *that*?" he asked respectfully.

"She said it *twice*," Laurie said. "Charles told her to say it *twice*."

"What happened to Charles?" my husband asked.

"Nothing," Laurie said. "He was passing out the crayons."

Monday morning Charles abandoned the little girl and said the evil word himself three or four times, getting his mouth washed out with soap each time. He also threw chalk.

My husband came to the door with me that evening as I set out for the P.T.A. meeting. "Invite her over for a cup of tea after the meeting," he said. "I want to get a look at her."

"If only she's there," I said prayerfully.

"She'll be there," my husband said. "I don't see how they could hold a P.T.A. meeting without Charles's mother."

At the meeting I sat restlessly, scanning each comfortable matronly face, trying to determine which one hid the secret of Charles. None of them looked to me haggard enough. No one stood up in the meeting and apologized for the way her son had been acting. No one mentioned Charles.

After the meeting, I sought out Laurie's kindergarten teacher. She had a plate with a cup of tea and a piece of chocolate cake. I had a plate with a cup of tea and a piece of marshmallow cake. We maneuvered up to one another cautiously, and smiled.

"I've been so anxious to meet you," I said. "I'm Laurie's mother."

"We are all so interested in Laurie," she said.

"Well, he certainly likes kindergarten," I said. "He talks about it all the time."

"We had a little trouble adjusting the first week or so," she said primly, "but now he's a fine little helper. With occasional lapses, of course."

"Laurie adjusts very quickly," I said. "I suppose this time it's Charles's influence."

"Charles?"

"Yes," I said, laughing, "you must have your hands full in that kindergarten with Charles."

"Charles?" she said. "We don't have any Charles in the kindergarten."

The Taming of the Shrew

*adapted by Regan Oaks from
the play by William Shakespeare*

*SHE'D SOONER SPIT IN A AN'S EYE THAN GIVE HIM
A KISS ON THE CHEEK. COULD PETRUCHIO TAME
THE TERRIBLE-TEMPERED KATE?*

Katherine the cursed, Katherine the shrew. She was one of the nastiest, bossiest, meanest women in all of Padua, with a tongue as sharp as a dagger, a temper as hot as the sun, and fists as hard as stone. Not only is this Kate cursed with a terrible disposition, she is cursed with a father who doesn't know *what* to do with her. And her father is cursed because no man will marry Kate and take her off his hands.

Ah, but here is Bianca. Sweet. Gentle. Loved by all. She, too, is cursed because her father will allow her no suitors until the fearsome Kate is married.

Screaming erupts from one of the windows in the Minola household. Neighbors passing by flinch nervously as if expecting things to come flying out at them. They hear the crash of splintering wood, and they quickly hide in the doorways. Oh, yes. This is not the first time they have witnessed such a temper tantrum.

In the room above, two women circle each other, the younger trying to avoid the flying arms of the older. "Sister, I know you have many suitors," Kate argues. "Tell me, tell me NOW, which one you like the best." She grabs Bianca's arm and twists it behind her back. Bianca tries to squirm free.

"Sister! Please let me go. I swear I have not yet seen that special face with which I could fancy myself in love."

"You lie. What of Hortensio? He flutters near you like a love-struck bat. Don't tell *me* you don't love *him*." She jerks Bianca's arms.

"I swear," the younger sister cries out in pain. "If you love Hortensio, sister, just tell me so and I shall speak to him for you."

"That mealymouthed potato!? I'd as soon be courted by a sack of flour! But I know there is someone—I can see it in your eyes."

There *is* a man, but Bianca does not know his name. She's seen him only that morning in the streets of Padua, his pale blue eyes capturing hers for a long, thrilling moment. Kate is watching Bianca closely and sees the dreamy look come into her eye again.

"I knew it!" she shouts viciously. "You are the reason Father wishes to marry me off to any cad who will have me." She twists Bianca's arms again.

"Sister, Kate, untie my hands!" Bianca cries.

Baptista rushes into the room and pulls Kate away from her prey. "Bianca, poor child," he coos. "Have nothing more to do with her. Leave the room." The girl flees. Now Baptista turns to devilish Kate. "Why do you wrong her that has never done wrong to you? Why must I have a daughter who is all nails and vinegar?"

Kate backs away as tears fill her eyes. "Bianca is your treasure. Everything is done for her. She must have a husband, but I must dance barefoot on her wedding day as old maids do!" She storms from the room.

Baptista sighs. "Was ever a father as cursed as I?"

Meanwhile, a tall, well-built man named Petruchio has come to Padua in search of a wife. Although he is a wealthy noble, his behavior is as rough as his clothing. As he walks down the street, he spots his friend Hortensio. "What ho!" he booms. "Hortensio, how goes it?"

Petruchio gives Hortensio a hardy whack on the back. The poor man tumbles and half chokes. "Why, Petruchio, how . . . how . . what brings you to our fair city?"

"My father has died, and I need someone to set the house in order. Do you know a single woman with a large dowry? I have decided to give myself a rich wife."

Hortensio's eyes light up. If he can drop Katherine into Petruchio's lap, a grateful Baptista just might let him have Bianca for his own wife. "There is such a woman. But, no, you are too much a friend for me to wish her on you."

Petruchio is not put off. "She can look like a dog for all I care—as long as she is wealthy."

Again Hortensio thinks. *Give him enough gold, and he'd marry a hag without a tooth in her head.* Now he smiles at his friend. "Well, this one is wealthy *and* beautiful, but her voice would make a cannon quiver."

"You don't know gold's effect. Tell me her name. I will marry her even if she sounds like all the heaven's thunder."

Secretly, Hortensio's own heart thrills. What luck this has been, after all, to meet Petruchio this morning. He puts his arm on his friend's shoulder and leads him down the street. "Come, I will take you to her father."

Also walking the streets of Padua that day is a young student named Lucentio. His head is also filled with marriage, but love, not gold, moves him. He has discovered the name of the girl he had seen just that morning. Bianca. Oh, she has such lovely eyes! Now he connives a way to meet her. He confesses to his servant, "Tranio, I *must* find her. The mere sight of her has stunned my soul."

"Is it possible to fall in love so fast?"

"I never thought so, but now it has happened to me. I saw her coral lips, her face so sweet and mild . . . she must be mine."

Tranio knows the woman and her father. He knows, too, that Baptista seeks a schoolmaster to instruct his daughters at home. He will not let Bianca go to school, where she might attract even more moonstruck lads. All this he confides to his master. Lucentio claps his hands. "Why, then, it's settled. I shall go to the house and present myself as a schoolmaster. I shall gain entry not just to the house but to Bianca's heart. Tranio, you are a genius!"

And so it happens that two gentlemen approach Baptista's house. Petruchio is about to knock on the door when Lucentio appears. The men nod to one another and exchange good morrows and something more . . . their reasons for coming. Petruchio agrees to recommend Lucentio as a schoolmaster for young Bianca, but only because it will further his own cause. Once inside, Baptista welcomes them. Before anyone can speak, Petruchio steps forward and makes his business quite clear.

"I hear you have a daughter, fair and virtuous, named Katherine," he says.

"I have a daughter named Katherine" is Baptista's honest answer.

"Having heard her praised for her beauty and gentle character—" He clears his throat to disguise a snicker. "I've come to look her over and see if she's a proper wife for me."

Baptista frowns. "I fear, sir, that my daughter is *not* for you."

"You wish not to part with her?"

"Well, no, it's just . . ."

Lucentio has been tugging on Petruchio's sleeve. "Tell him. Tell him why I am here."

"Oh, yes," Petruchio says. "I have brought a tutor for your daughter. Will you accept him as a token of my esteem?"

"With pleasure," Baptista beams.

"Well, then. My time runs short. I cannot come to woo every day. If I win your daughter's love, what dowry comes with her?"

"At my death, half my lands. And for the present, twenty thousand gold pieces," Baptista says.

Petruchio smiles. "Quite acceptable. When I die, I shall leave all my land and leases to her. Shall we draw up the contract?"

Baptista is not so easily won. He knows Katherine's fiery temperament. To win her love may be impossible, but he insists that Petruchio try.

"*Father*," Petruchio says, moving closer to the man, "I woo roughly, not like a child. I will be as strong as she is headstrong. So send her to me, and I shall pick your sweet Kate from the tree of love."

Baptista shakes his head doubtfully. His Katherine is not *sweet*. Nevertheless, he leads Lucentio from the room to meet Bianca. Alone now, Petruchio plots his courtship. If the shrew frowns, then he'll say she smiles. If she bids him to go, then he'll thank her for begging him to stay. If she refuses to marry, he'll simply set the wedding date.

Just then, the door flies open and Kate bursts into the room. For a moment, Petruchio is taken aback. Her hair is a tangled mess; her eyes burn with anger. Quickly, Petruchio recovers his confidence and speaks in a loud, boastful voice. "Here you are. Good morrow, Kate, for that's your name, I hear."

"Then you're hard of hearing. Those who talk to me call me Katherine."

"You lie, for you are called plain Kate, or bonny Kate, or sometimes Kate the cursed. But to me you are the fairest Kate, and I have come to make you my wife."

Her eyes pierce him. "Let him that brought you here remove you hence."

"Nay, Kate. Come sit on my lap." He sits down and slaps his knee, then reaches for her. She pulls away. "What?" Petruchio laughs. "You are not too heavy for a man such as I. You are light."

"Too light for you to catch!" she snaps.

Petruchio feels his confidence slipping. "Come, you buzzing wasp. You are too angry."

"If I be waspish, then you'd best beware my sting!" she warns.

"Ah." Petruchio nods, then stands. "The way to handle a wasp is to swat it."

Kate is alarmed. She moves behind a chair. "Get out."

"I am a gentleman," he says as he moves toward her. She slaps his face. Shocked, he stares a moment and then responds. "I swear I'll cuff you if you strike again."

"Then you are no gentleman," she replies. She has won the point.

Petruchio puts out his arms. "Come, don't look so sour. I am a husband who suits you." He closes his arms around her and they struggle.

"Let me go!" She stomps her foot upon his. "Let me go, you oaf!"

Still struggling, Petruchio makes light of the game. "Ah, such sweet words. I was told you were rough and sullen, but I find you warm and pleasant, if a bit slow in the mind."

"Slow in the mind!?" she shouts.

"I like you well enough," Petruchio continues. "So, now down to business. Your father has agreed to our wedding and your dowry. Like it or not, we shall marry, for I was born to tame you, Kate, and make you mine. Here comes your father. I shall give him our joyous news."

Baptista enters the room reluctantly. "How goes it?" he asks, though he thinks he already knows. To his surprise, Petruchio announces the wedding will take place.

"I'll see you hanged first," Kate spits.

Petruchio ignores her. "Those who have talked ill of my fine Kate have talked amiss. She is not mean or cursed but as gentle as a cooing dove. We have got along so well that Sunday is our wedding date."

Kate succeeds in pulling free. She reaches for a stool and raises it above her head. "I'll crack you with this if you come near me again!"

Petruchio laughs. "We agreed that she would still seem cursed in company. But when we were alone, she was a fountain of affection. She kissed me until my heart could resist no longer. So, now, good-bye. I must be off to buy my wedding clothes."

He hurries from the room, leaving a stunned Kate and a bewildered Baptista behind.

The wedding day has arrived, but the bridegroom has not. Dressed in a gown of finest silk as befits a gentlewoman, Kate has been sitting at the altar all afternoon. The guests are nodding off in the pews. Needless to say, the bride-to-be is not pleased.

"I am forced to marry this clod, this dolt, this pile of ill manners, for the sake of my father—no, for my sister's sake. It is her happiness you care about, not mine! I *hate* men," she says.

Just then, Petruchio enters the church looking more like a collector of junk than a bridegroom. His shirt is in rags; his breeches are patched; his sword is rusty; why, not even his boots match! But he is not in the least apologetic. "Ah, Father, is the bride ready to claim her prize?"

Baptista is angry. "I can't believe you have come to your wedding dressed like that!"

Petruchio cares not. "Is Kate marrying me or my clothes?" He leans closer and whispers, "Remember, once she is mine, she is out of your house—and hair—forever."

Baptista nods. "Quite so. Quite so. Come, then; your beloved is waiting."

Petruchio takes his place beside a fuming Kate. The priest quickly says the marriage vows that unite the two lovebirds. At once, Petruchio takes Kate's hand and begins to drag her down the aisle. "Come quickly. We're due home tonight."

She resists. "The wedding feast is about to begin. I will not go today, nor tomorrow. I will go when it pleases me."

"Kate," he says firmly, "we go now."

"I see a woman may be a fool if she has not the spirit to resist. Come, everyone, to the bridal dinner."

Petruchio also addresses the wedding guests. "Obey the bride. Go to the feast. Be mad and merry to your heart's content. But, as for my bonny Kate, she must go with me." He looks into her fiery eyes. "Do not look sour nor stamp nor fret. I will be master of what is my own. You are my goods, my house, my horse, my anything. I command you, *come!*"

So saying, Petruchio seizes Kate by the arm and drags her kicking and screaming from the chapel. He loads her onto a horse, then swings onto his own. Bride and groom set out on the journey to Verona.

"Food, food, food!" Petruchio shouts at his servants upon his arrival at home. "Where is my supper?" The servants gaze at each other in shock, then scurry about like rabbits. Exhausted, Katherine flinches with each loud boom of her husband's voice. "Where is my wine? Can't you see my wife has a stomach and is hungry? Come, knaves, serve your new mistress."

The servants march out with piles of food—roasted chickens, fruits, and wines. Petruchio glares at the tray of chicken. "This meat is burnt! Where is that rascal cook!"

Kate is famished, but as she reaches for a drumstick, Petruchio seizes it first and hurls it at the feet of a servant. "You beetle-headed, flop-eared fool. This food is unfit for a dog, let alone my new bride. Take it all away!"

"Husband," Kate speaks weakly. "Be not so disquiet. The meat was good."

"I tell you it was burnt. My love, we shall fast tonight, and tomorrow we'll eat. Come, it's time for sleep."

"What, did you marry me to famish me?" she argues.

So goes Petruchio's strategy. Kate has eaten no meat on this day, nor shall she eat meat tomorrow. He'll find fault with the bed and throw off the covers and the sheets so that she cannot sleep upon it. And he'll do it all in professing his love for her. This is the way to kill a wife with kindness, he thinks. He who knows better how to tame a shrew, let him speak.

Four weeks have passed, four weeks in which Kate has been constantly amazed by the wildness of her husband. Every time she acts shrewish, he acts crazier. She's lost weight and is beginning to think twice before she blows up at him. When word arrives, however, that Lucentio and her sister Bianca will wed, Kate feels happiness. She will return for the wedding feast, but suddenly she frowns. What will Petruchio do this time to sour the day? To her surprise, her husband agrees to attend the festivities. Furthermore, he tells her he has a surprise. At once, Kate is wary. She's already had a good dose of her husband's surprises. He takes her hand. "Come, my love. I'll show you."

He leads Kate into a nearby room. She stands amazed at what she sees—beautiful clothes laid out. A tailor bows to them. She lifts a stylish new cap and hugs it to her. Once more, however, her husband's smiles have turned to frowns. "What is this?" he shouts at the tailor. "Do you call this a cap?"

"It is what you asked me to make," answers the confused tailor.

"This is a rag. Take it away. I want a larger one for my love to wear."

"Love me or love me not!" Kate protests. "I like the cap, and I will have it or I will have none!"

"Then you shall have none." Petruchio takes the cap and stomps on it. He turns and looks at the gown. "This sleeve, these pleats . . . you would have my wife look piggish?!" He tears the fabric as Kate watches in dismay. Then he turns to her. "These fine clothes are not good enough for you. We shall go to the wedding in our simple clothes."

"But a gentlewoman does not dress—"

Petruchio interrupts her. "Is the jay more precious than the lark because his feathers are more beautiful?" he asks. "No. Don't you understand, your beauty is not in your gentlewoman's clothes?"

Kate stares at him a moment. Does he speak the truth this time? Is she beautiful? she wonders.

Petruchio turns away. "If you're embarrassed before your family, then blame me."

On the morning of the wedding day, Petruchio and Katherine, accompanied by their servants, ride along a public road to Padua. "How bright and goodly shines the moon," Petruchio comments.

"The moon! No, it is the sun that shines," Kate corrects him.

"I say it is the moon."

"It is the *sun!*" she argues.

"It is the moon, or the star, or whatever I say or else," Petruchio warns, "or I shall ride no farther and we shall return to Verona."

Katherine longs to visit with her family. And so, she gives in. "It is the moon."

Petruchio grins. "You lie. It is the blessed sun."

Katherine is exasperated. But she holds her tongue and eyes her husband. She understands now the game. "Then God be blessed," she answers sweetly. "Have it what you will. Moon, sun, whatever Petruchio says it is, so it will be for Katherine."

Petruchio is much pleased. He has won the field, or so he thinks. And yet he tests Kate still. Outside her father's home in Padua, he refuses to go a step further until Katherine gives him a kiss. She is shocked. "What? In the middle of the street?"

"Are you ashamed of me?" he asks.

Kate smiles. She has not quit playing the game. But she has learned to play it differently, to her advantage. "Goodness, no!" she says, sweetness once more upon her tongue. "But ashamed of kissing in public? Yes. It is not a gentlewoman's behavior."

Petruchio throws up his hands and declares that they will not enter Baptista's home but shall return to Verona.

"Wait!" she says. "I will give thee a kiss." She leans forward and gently presses her lips on his nose.

"You call that a kiss? I'd rather a peck from a chicken!"

"And I from a rooster," she laughs. "But I did kiss you

and now we must enter the house." And so she does, leaving a disquieted Petruchio to follow.

After the wedding ceremony, Katherine visits with her sister Bianca while the men eat and drink and talk of their wives. Hortensio has also married within the last few weeks. His wife is a wealthy widow. Now he nudges Petruchio in the ribs and asks, "I have never seen Katherine so quiet. How goes it with you? Have you tamed the shrew?"

"I'll wager a bet that my wife will attend to me quicker than yours, or even *yours*, Lucentio."

The bridegroom laughs and both he and Hortensio agree to the bet. Lucentio begins the test. He orders a servant to tell Bianca that her husband bids her to come to him. The servant leaves and returns with Bianca's answer. "She says to tell you she is otherwise occupied," the servant says.

Lucentio frowns. Petruchio grins. Now it is Hortensio's turn. He stands and says to his servant, "Entreat my wife to come to me forthwith."

"Ooooh," Petruchio mocks him. "Entreat! There is a powerful word. She ought to come running."

The servant returns without the widow. "Master, your wife says if you have something to tell her, then you should come to her."

Petruchio laughs. Now it is his turn. "Servant, tell my Katherine that I *command* her to come to me."

The servant gulps, for he remembers well Kate the cursed. He hurries away. Moments later, wild screaming bursts from the women's quarters. Petruchio's face falls. He has been too boastful. His Katherine has tricked him. But no sooner have Lucentio and Hortensio begun to count their winnings when Katherine enters, dragging with her the other two wives. Petruchio's face lights up at once with pleasure.

"Bianca," Katherine scolds her sister. "Obey your husband's honest wishes. He cares for you. It is your duty to care for him."

"Duty?" Bianca cries. "It's a fool's duty."

"Is it?" asks Lucentio. "Your lack of duty has just cost me one hundred pounds."

"Who is the fool—I or you for making such a bet?" she snaps.

"Is this our sweet Bianca?" asks Petruchio. "My, my, my."

Katherine gently advises her sister. "Unknot your brow. Do not wound your husband, your lord, with your mean looks. It blots your beauty as frost mottles the buds. Your husband desires no other reward for caring and warming and feeding you than kindness. It is little payment. I was once like you, Bianca, throwing word for word, frown for frown. But I see now that my lances were but straws." She reaches her hand to Petruchio, who takes it. Her words have surprised even him.

"There's a good wife, Kate. Come and kiss me."

Until now, the only kiss she has freely given him has been the chicken peck upon his nose an hour earlier. Now she kisses him fully on the lips.

Hortensio stares. "My eyes tell me what I have just seen, but my brain stumbles in disbelief. He has tamed the shrew!"

Bianca, too, stares in disbelief. Then, contrite, she puts her hand in Lucentio's. "Love's lesson is clear. We must attend each other, care for each other, make our two separate selves into one."

For once, Baptista's household is peaceful.

The Punishment

adapted from the novel Jane Eyre
by Charlotte Brontë

JANE EYRE HAD LOST HER PARENTS AND WAS AT THE
MERCY OF THOSE DETERMINED TO BREAK HER SPIRIT.

There was no possibility of taking a walk that day. A bitter November storm had brought with it clouds so somber and a rain so penetrating that outdoor exercise was out of the question. I was glad of it. I never liked long walks, especially on chilly afternoons. Dreadful to me was the coming home in the raw twilight, with nipped fingers and toes, and a heart saddened by the chidings of Bessie, the nurse, and the reminders of my inferiority to my cousins: Eliza, John, and Georgiana Reed.

Outside the rain lashed across the meadow. Inside the stone walls of Gateshead Hall, my Aunt Reed reclined on a sofa by the fireside in the drawing room. Clustered around her were her little darlings. I stood in the doorway, uninvited. "Until Bessie tells me that you are behaving like a lady, Jane, I don't want you near my children," Mrs.

Reed said. "A warm fire is a privilege intended only for contented, happy little children."

"What does Bessie say I have done?" I asked.

"Jane, I don't like cavilers or questioners. Be seated somewhere. And until you can talk pleasantly, remain silent."

A small breakfast room adjoined the drawing room. I slipped in there. I selected a book from a shelf and sat cross-legged on the window seat. Books were more interesting to me than my spoiled cousins anyway. This volume was Bewick's *History of British Birds*. Each picture told a story. With the book on my knee, I was happy. I feared nothing but interruption, and that came too soon. The breakfast room door opened.

"Madam Mope!" cried the voice of John Reed. He found the room empty. In fact, a scarlet window drapery hid me, with my legs tucked up, from his view. "Where the dickens is she?"

I wished John Reed would not discover my hiding place. But just then Eliza came into the room. "She's in the window seat, to be sure, Jack," she told her brother.

I came out immediately, for I trembled at the idea of being dragged forth by John Reed. "What do you want?" I asked.

"Say 'What do you want, Master Reed'" was his answer. "I want you to come here." He sat himself in an armchair and waited.

John Reed was a schoolboy of fourteen years, four years older than I. He was large and stout for his age, with a dingy and unwholesome skin. He gorged himself habitually at the table, which gave him dim eyes and flabby cheeks. He bullied me and punished me, not two or three times in the week, nor once or twice in the day, but continually. Every nerve in my body feared him. Every morsel of flesh on my bones shrank when he came near. At times, the terror he inspired bewildered me and I wondered at it. I walked toward his chair, as commanded.

All at once without speaking, he struck suddenly and strongly. I tottered from his slap and stepped back. "That is for talking back to Mama a while ago—and for the insulting look in your eye just now, you rat!"

I had always endured his abuse. I did so now.

"What were you doing behind the curtain?" he asked.

"I was reading."

"Show me the book."

I fetched it from the window seat.

"You have no business to take our books. You are a dependent, Mama says. You have no money. Your father left you none. You ought to beg and not live here with gentlemen's children like us and eat the same meals we do and wear clothes at our Mama's expense. Now, I'll teach you to rummage my bookshelves, for these books are mine. All the house belongs to me, or will in a few years. Go and stand by the door, out of the way of the mirror and the windows."

I did so, not aware of what his intention was. He raised the book and flung. It struck me and I fell forward, gashing my forehead against the sharp edge of the wood frame. My fingers felt blood. Suddenly, my terror had passed its climax and another emotion took its place. "You are wicked and cruel!" I screamed. "You are like a . . . a murderer!"

John Reed ran headlong at me. He grasped my hair. I swung my fists and knuckled him in the face.

"You rat! You rat!" he bellowed.

Bessie rushed into the room. Eliza had run for Mrs. Reed, and now she too entered the room. When the servants parted us, I saw that John Reed was bleeding from his nose. I was bloody, too, from the gash on my head. "Dear, dear!" cried Bessie. "What a fury to fly at Master John!" she scolded.

"Take her away to the red room and lock her in there," Mrs. Reed's cold voice commanded.

At once, four hands were laid upon me. Bessie and Miss Abbott, the housekeeper, led me upstairs. I resisted all the way. Bessie and Miss Abbott thrust me, still kicking, into a chair. "You are like a mad cat! What shocking conduct, Miss Eyre, to strike your young master."

"Master!" I cried. "How is he my master? Am I a servant?"

"If you don't sit still, I will tie you down."

"No, please don't!"

My anger still boiled, but I forced myself to sit still. Tears and blood streaked my face. Miss Abbott breathed a little easier and stepped away from me, but not before calling me a disgusting toad. When Bessie spoke again, her voice was kinder. "What I tell you now is for your own good. You are not of equal standing with your cousins. Your Aunt Reed was very kind to allow you to stay here after your mama and papa died."

"Only because Uncle Reed made her promise to take care of me," I whimpered. "Oh, Bessie, why did he have to die, too?"

"I don't know, child. But crying will do you no good. And if Mrs. Reed turns you out, you will be in the poorhouse."

"God will punish you," said Miss Abbott in a voice cold and sharp. "He might strike you dead in the midst of your tantrums, and then where will you go? Behave yourself, Miss Eyre, or something bad will come down that chimney and fetch you away!"

They left, locking the door behind them.

The red room was a spare chamber, very seldom slept in. Yet it was one of the largest rooms in the mansion. Curtains of deep red damask covered the windows. The room was cold because it seldom had a fire and did not have one burning in the grate now. I stared at the mouth of the fireplace and shivered, more from fear than from cold. What exactly might come down the chimney and steal me away? I looked at the bed piled high now with pillows like a throne. In that very bed my kind Uncle Reed had died. I remembered the candles burning and people crying. No candles burned now. As the day was ending, the faint light that came through the long windows grew dimmer.

At first, I was too terrified to move. In time, though, I stood and went to the door. I pulled on the knob, but no jail was more secure. They had indeed locked me inside. How long would they keep me here? Would they starve me to death? I lifted my head and tried to look boldly around the room. At that moment, a light gleamed on the wall. From where did it come? The sky beyond the windows was black now, and no moonlight shown through the glass. My heart beat thick; my head grew hot; a sound filled my ears, which I deemed the rushing of wings. Something seemed near me. I was suffocating. I rushed to the door and shook the lock desperately.

"Bessie!" I screamed. "Help me! Let me out, let me out!"

The lock turned. The door opened. "What a dreadful noise!" said Bessie.

"Take me out! Let me go into the nursery," was my cry.

"What? Are you hurt?"

"I saw a light, a ghost. It's in the room." I grabbed Bessie's hand and would not let go.

Mrs. Reed came down the hall. "What is this? I gave orders for her to be locked inside."

"But she screamed so frightfully, ma'am," Bessie objected.

"It is an act. I detest antics in the young. She will stay in the red room until I come for her."

"Oh, Aunt," I pleaded. "Have pity. Forgive me. Please! Punish me some other way. I shall be killed if—"

"Silence!" She abruptly thrust me back and locked me in.

"No, don't leave me alone!" I heard her sweeping away, and soon after she was gone, I suppose I took a sort of fit. A great gust of wind howled down the chimney. The next instant, I crumpled to the floor.

The next thing I remember is waking up with a feeling as if I had had a frightful nightmare. I heard voices, too, speaking with hollow sounds. Before long, I became aware that someone was handling me, lifting me up and supporting me in a sitting posture, and doing so more tenderly than I had ever been held before. I rested my head against the arm and felt easy.

In five minutes more, the cloud of bewilderment dissolved. I knew quite well then that I was in my own bed. It was night. A candle burned on the table. Bessie stood at the bed-foot with a basin in her hand, and a gentleman sat in a chair near my pillow, leaning over me. I recognized him as Dr. Lloyd. "Well, you have been crying, Miss Jane," he said. "Have you any pain?"

"She had a fall, Doctor," Bessie explained.

"I was knocked down," I said.

"Is that what made you ill?" the doctor asked kindly.

"I was shut up in a room where there is a ghost."

"Really, Miss Jane." Bessie laughed. "Are you such a baby, afraid of ghosts?"

A bell rang for the servants' dinner. Dr. Lloyd turned to Bessie. "That bell is for you, nurse. Go down. I'll give Miss Jane a lecture till you come back."

Bessie would have preferred to stay, but she did not want to anger Mrs. Reed. When the nurse had gone, Dr. Lloyd asked, "Don't you think Gateshead Hall is a very beautiful place?"

"It is not my house, sir," the girl said. "I don't like it here, not at all."

"But you have a kind aunt and cousins to play with," he said.

"It was John Reed who knocked me down and my aunt who locked me inside the room with no fire and no light."

Dr. Lloyd frowned. "Have you any other relations besides Mrs. Reed?"

"I asked Mrs. Reed once. She said possibly I had some poor, low relations called Eyre, but they were beggars and she will have nothing to do with them."

"How would you like to go away to school, Jane?"

I scarcely knew what school was. Bessie sometimes spoke of it as a place where young ladies sat in the stocks, wrote on slate boards, and were expected to be exceedingly genteel and precise. John Reed hated school and abused his master, but John Reed's tastes were no rule for mine. The thought of leaving Gateshead and John Reed forever made me smile. "I would like that very much."

"Well, well, who knows what may happen?" said Dr. Lloyd. "The child ought to have a change of air and scene," he added, speaking to himself. "Nerves not in a good state."

Next day, by noon, I was up and dressed, and sat wrapped in a shawl by the nursery hearth. I felt physically weak and broken down. But my worst ailment was an unutterable wretchedness of mind. No sooner had I wiped one salt drop from my cheek than another tear followed. Yet, I thought, I ought to have been happy, for none of the Reeds was there to torment me. They were all gone out in the carriage with their mama. Miss Abbott was in the sewing room with Bessie, and I heard them speaking about me.

"Poor Miss Jane is to be pitied," Bessie spoke.

"If she were a nice, pretty child, one might feel sorry for her forlornness. But one really cannot care for such a plain little toad as she," Abbott answered.

"You would feel differently if it were Miss Georgiana who had been so cruelly punished."

"Oh, I dote on Miss Georgiana!" cried the fervent Abbott. "Little darling!—with her long curls and her blue eyes, and such a sweet color as she has, just as if she were a beautiful painting."

A child can feel, but she has difficulty understanding her feelings. Why was I always suffering, always browbeaten, always accused? Why could I never please? Eliza was headstrong and selfish but respected. Georgiana was spoiled and boastful but indulged. Her beauty, her pink cheeks and golden curls, gave delight to all who looked upon her. Even John Reed, who twisted the necks of pigeons and pinched off the buds of roses, was still Mrs. Reed's "darling."

In the days and weeks that passed, I thought often of school though no one mentioned it to me again. Mrs. Reed ordered me to eat my meals alone. Still, John Reed prowled about outside my room. "Stay away from her," Mrs. Reed told him. "She is not worthy of our notice."

I could not help myself. "Your little darlings are not fit to be with *me*!" I answered.

Mrs. Reed was upon me instantly. She grabbed my shoulders and shook me soundly, then boxed my ears. "You are to stay in your room the rest of the day. I do not want to even hear your voice!"

"What would Uncle Reed say if he were alive?" I cried. "He is in heaven with my mama and papa, and they see all you do and think, and they know how you shut me up all day long and how you wish me dead, too!"

I saw something like fear flicker in Mrs. Reed's eyes. She let me go and hurried away.

November, December, and half of January passed. Christmas and the New Year had been celebrated at Gateshead with the usual festive cheer. Presents had been interchanged, dinners and evening parties given. From every enjoyment I was excluded, though the other children were not. Pretty Georgiana in her party dresses danced and curtsied for the happy guests. Though somewhat sad, I was not miserable. To speak truth, I did not wish to go into their company, for in their company I was rarely noticed. I sat alone in my room with my doll on my knee. When the fire got low, I glanced fearfully around the room for the ghost I had seen in the red room, then quickly hurried to my bed.

One morning, Bessie came to me in quite a hurry. She hauled me to the washbasin and scrubbed my face and hands with soap, water, and a coarse towel. I was wanted, she told me, in the breakfast room, and I was to behave myself. I went down the stairs and stopped before the closed door. I was trembling. The violent ringing of the breakfast room bell summoned me. I *must* enter.

Mrs. Reed sat in her usual chair near the fire. In the room with her was a strange man who turned his head slowly and examined me with two gray eyes under a pair of bushy brows. "Her size is small," he said. "What is her age?"

"Ten years."

"Your name, little girl?"

"Jane Eyre, sir." I looked up. He seemed to me a tall gentleman, but then I was very little.

"Well, Jane Eyre, are you a good child?"

It was impossible to answer yes, for Mrs. Reed was always telling me I was not good. Mrs. Reed answered for me now. "Perhaps the less said on that subject the better, Mr. Brocklehurst."

"No sight is so sad as that of a naughty little girl." He stepped toward me. "Tell me, young lady, where do the wicked go after death?"

The questioned surprised me. "Why, they go to hell, sir."

"And what is that?"

"A pit of fire."

"And what must you do, Jane Eyre, to avoid this pit?"

I smiled. "Why, that's simple. I must stay healthy and never die!"

Mr. Brocklehurst's bushy eyebrows darted upward in surprise.

"You see how bold the child is?" Mrs. Reed complained. "The teachers at Lowood School had better keep an eye on her. She lies."

"A liar! How disgusting."

Uttered before a stranger, the accusation cut me to the heart. Mrs. Reed was poisoning my future. What was the good of going away if those who waited for me there believed the things Mrs. Reed told them about me? Already Mr. Brocklehurst was convinced I was a deceitful child.

"I wish her to be brought up in a manner suiting her prospects," continued Mrs. Reed, "to be made useful and humble. As for vacations, she will spend them always at Lowood. I will not have my children under the same roof with this beggar," Mrs. Reed added.

"I assure you, Mrs. Reed, that Jane Eyre will learn to take her humble place in the world and to serve others." He bowed politely and left.

Mrs. Reed and I were left alone. Some minutes passed in silence. She was sewing. I was watching her. Mrs. Reed looked up from her work. Her eyes settled on mine. "Go out of the room," she ordered coldly. "Return at once to the nursery."

I got up and went to the door, but there I stopped. The conversation that had just been spoken between Mrs. Reed and Mr. Brocklehurst was stinging in my mind. A passion of resentment flowed through me. *Speak* I must.

"I am not a liar," I said quite suddenly. "If I were, Aunt, I should say that I *love* you when I actually dislike you more than anyone in the world except John Reed."

Mrs. Reed sat still. Her eyes of ice dwelled on mine. "What more have you to say?"

That icy stare and that mean voice stirred my resentment even more. "I will never call you aunt again as long as I live. I will never come to see you when I am grown up, and if any one asks me how I liked you and how you treated me, I will say the very thought of you makes me sick and that you treated me with miserable cruelty."

"How dare you!"

"How dare I?" the girl repeated. "Because it is the truth. You think I have no feelings and that I can do without one bit of love or kindness, but I cannot live so."

Mrs. Reed appeared frightened. She rocked herself to and fro, about to cry. "Jane, dear, you are under a mistake. What is the matter with you? I care for you very much. Didn't I bring you into my own home?"

"I am not your *dear*. Send me away to Lowood very soon, Mrs. Reed, for I have no wish to live in this hateful house!"

"I will indeed send her to school soon," Mrs. Reed murmured. Gathering up her knitting, she left the room.

I was left there alone—winner of the field. It was the hardest battle I had fought, and the first victory I had ever gained. I stood awhile on the rug, enjoying my victory. First, I smiled to myself and felt elated. But this fierce pleasure subsided. I felt a pang of guilt. Children should not talk to their elders in such a way. I should go to her at once and apologize. I stood a wretched child, not knowing what to do.

Then I heard a clear voice call "Miss Jane! Where are you? Come to lunch!"

It was Bessie, but I did not stir. After my victory over Mrs. Reed, I no longer cared if Bessie was angry with me.

"Why don't you come when you are called?" she asked, stepping inside the breakfast room.

"I don't think I shall ever be afraid of you or Mrs. Reed again," I said. Never before had I spoken so bravely.

"You have a new way of speaking. What makes you so bold?"

"Knowing that I shall soon be away from here," I answered.

"You are a strange child, Miss Jane," she said. "I have often thought you should be bolder to those who would condemn you." She knelt before me. "I believe I am fonder of you than all the other children in this house."

"You don't show it."

"Will you be so glad to leave me?"

I looked at her and answered truthfully. "Just now I am rather sorry to be leaving you."

We embraced. That afternoon passed in peace and harmony. In the evening Bessie sang me sweet songs and told me enchanting stories. Even for me life had its gleams of sunshine.

Prometheus—Fire in the Mind

*A retelling of a Greek myth
by Kate Davis*

From the top of Mount Caucasus, Prometheus sees the first fiery arrows of dawn. They pierce the Titan's veins. "Bring back the night!" he cries to the gods on Mount Olympus. Only the cold blanket of darkness can restore his peace of mind. But the gods are not listening. Strange that Prometheus can feel anything at all. For centuries he has been chained to the granite mountain, and he knows that struggling is useless. Prometheus braces himself. He knows full well what follows the dawn. Out of the glowing light on the horizon the Great Tormentor comes. As she circles overhead on silent wings, Zeus's voice fills the space between heaven and Earth. "Apologize for your crime, and I will set you free."

"Never!"

"Then feel my torture!" Now Zeus commands his vulture: "Do your duty, winged hound!"

The bird dives. The next instant, it sinks its talons into human flesh and with its beak digs deep to taste the liver. Prometheus screams. And his scream echoes across the span of time. He is an immortal god, and so he cannot die. For a thousand years he has endured this forced exile. Each morning the vulture descends to eat his liver. Each night his liver grows anew. The only escape is in Prometheus's mind. He wanders the halls of memory and recalls the reason for his torment.

Long, long ago when the world was young, the ruler of Mount Olympus was Cronus. But Cronus was insane—and horrid. The wretched ruler feared they would take over his throne someday. And so he devoured his sons. Only Zeus survived, and when he came of age, Zeus fulfilled the prophecy. He banded with the young gods on Mount Olympus to wage war against Cronus.

The war of the Titans caused the very heavens to quake. Storms exploded with the force of their blows. Lightning flared with the clash of their weapons. Thunder roared with their groans. Finally, because of Prometheus's wise help, Zeus defeated the elders. He crowned himself the supreme ruler and took his place on the throne upon Mount Olympus.

One day, Zeus summoned Prometheus. "Bring your young brother Epimetheus," he commanded. When they appeared before him, Zeus sighed, "I am bored. I can throw thunderbolts only so often. I have been contemplating a sort of game: the creation of humble immortals, humans, to amuse and to praise me."

"What of animals?" suggested Epimetheus. "Lions and snakes might make the game a bit more exciting."

"Yes," nodded Zeus. "And you shall create them." Then he turned to Prometheus. "I leave the humans to you."

Epimetheus did as he was commanded. "Come forth, lions and bats!" he called. "Slither forward, snakes and lizards! Fly in, eagles and wrens!"

One by one, Epimetheus dealt the beasts fur and feathers, fangs and wings. He gave them all kinds of qualities—speed or strength to some; cunning or gentleness to others. When he had exhausted his gifts, he turned to his brother. "Prometheus, I have given away too much," he fretted. "There is nothing left for you to grant to the human players."

"You think not," Prometheus replied. "But give me a moment, and I'll devise the most extraordinary of all gifts."

Prometheus scooped soft clay from the riverbed and shaped a new figure. He molded legs so that they could walk and appear dignified. He gave them tools—clubs, bows, bone knives. When he was finished, he brought the humans before Zeus.

"Fine work," Zeus admitted. "What will these mortals sacrifice to me to thank me for creating them?"

I have created the clay figures, Prometheus wanted to

protest, but he kept his thoughts silent. He was rather fond of the clay figures he had sculpted—more fond, indeed, than of any reward he might receive from Zeus for completing the task. And so Prometheus gave Zeus a choice. First, he butchered an ox and separated the meat from the bones, the fat from the gristle. In one bag he packed the meat with gristle on top. In the other, he packed the bones with the fat on top. Then he hauled the bags before Zeus.

"Which offering do you prefer?" Prometheus asked him. The god of thunderbolts was brawny and powerful, but Prometheus had learned that Zeus was not skilled at looking beneath the surface of things.

"Hmmm." Zeus wet his lips as he made up his mind. "The richest, juiciest portion, of course," he said. He chose the glistening bag of fat. "The humans may keep the other sack," he said. This was what Prometheus had expected. His humble humans would feast on meat and offer only the fat and bones to Zeus as a token of their devotion.

Zeus saw that he had been tricked. "Keep your mortals in line, and teach them how to provide for themselves, for I won't be handing out any miracles. And under no circumstances are they to borrow my fire!"

Once alone, Prometheus said to his brother, "Do you see what he is doing? By keeping fire from humans, Zeus denies them warmth and the means to forge weapons."

"If humans stay ignorant," the brother reasoned, "they will pose no threat to Zeus?"

"Precisely," said Prometheus. "But what's worst of all,"

he added, "Zeus withholds the flames of inspiration."

That night while Zeus slept, Prometheus crept into the halls of Mount Olympus. Silently, he made his way past rows of towering white columns. He came to the great Fountain of Fire, the ever-burning font from which Zeus lit his thunderbolts. Prometheus stirred the coals. He chose the brightest one and dropped it into a hollow reed he'd brought with him. Wrapping the reed carefully, he concealed it in his garments. Then he stole quickly back the way he'd come.

As he passed Zeus's chambers, however, he caught sight of a golden box gleaming in the corner. *Ah!* he realized, *this must be where Zeus keeps his defenses hidden. Inside that box are all the plagues and terrors of the world!* Prometheus unwrapped the fire coal and chipped off a tiny chunk. Gingerly, he cracked open the box and dropped the spark inside. Then he descended to Earth.

When Zeus rose from his bed, he saw hundreds of fires sparking on Earth. Looking closer, he detected a certain new brilliance shining in the eyes of the humans.

"SOMEONE HAS STOLEN MY FIRE!" he bellowed. His voice split the ground with earthquakes.

The humans cringed and cowered in their caves. Prometheus stood bold and replied with more wisdom than Zeus could grasp. "Your storms may extinguish the humans' heat and light, but you will never put out the fire in their minds!"

Zeus called his aides Force and Violence. "What does he mean?"

Violence spoke first. "It doesn't matter. Prometheus

has disobeyed you, and he must be punished. Smash him!"

"Yes! Yes!" Zeus was seething with anger. He summoned his blacksmith, Hephaestus, to his side. "Make me a chain," he ordered. "Make it as strong as my fury. Drag it, along with hammer and stakes, to Mount Caucasus. Force and Violence will meet you there with a prisoner."

"What then?" Hephaestus asked.

"Find the highest outcropping, and shackle my prisoner to the rocks. Leave him exposed to shrivel in the sun, to freeze in the cold, and to be preyed upon by vultures—forever!"

Hephaestus shuddered at such a fate and yet he knew better than to cross Zeus when he was angry. The blacksmith's crippled leg was evidence of Zeus's powerful blows. The blacksmith hurried away to begin the task.

Prometheus was clever, but no match for the twin powers of Force and Violence. They captured him and dragged him to the remote mountaintop.

"For your defiance against Zeus," gloated Violence, "you will be forever an outcast, tortured until the end of time."

"Is it a sin to help humans better themselves?" Prometheus tried to reason with Violence but to no avail.

When Hephaestus saw whom he was to chain, he nearly wept. "Prometheus, you are a god among gods. My heart is heavy with the task demanded of me. I have no courage to bind so noble a kinsman."

"Don't waste your pity," said Violence.

"Drive in the stake!" said Force.

"Do it," said Prometheus. "Or Zeus's wrath will fall on

your head."

"If only my craft were less perfect," Hephaestus lamented. "As it is, no weapon made by god or mortal—save Zeus's thunderbolts—can release you from this iron chain."

When Epimetheus heard what had happened to his brother, he flew to his side, wailing. He pounded the chains with a rock, but the rock shattered. "Stop," said Prometheus. "I have done what I was destined to do."

"I shall come every day to comfort you," vowed his loyal brother.

"No. Come no more. I forbid it. You must teach the mortals. Return to Earth and be their guide. Teach them about the stars. Flame the fires in their mind, but above all else, be wary of Zeus! He will try to deceive you."

Prometheus could not have been more correct. Zeus had not yet spent all his anger. He devised a way to punish the humans for accepting Prometheus's gift of fire. He created a mortal woman and called her Pandora. He modeled her after the most alluring goddesses on Mount Olympus. He schooled her in all the arts of persuasion and granted her an unquenchable curiosity. Then he gave Pandora her orders. "Go to Earth," he instructed. "Become the bride of Epimetheus. And," Zeus added, handing her a glorious golden case, "give him this for a wedding gift."

"Oh, Zeus!" she sighed. "It is so beautiful. What is inside?"

"Never," he warned her, "*never* open the box."

Pandora departed. The moment Epimetheus saw

Pandora, he fell in love. She charmed him with her beauty and with her laughter like sunshine. They married. Zeus had set in motion his revenge, and now he bided his time. Before long, Pandora's curiosity overwhelmed her. While Epimetheus was tending his flocks, she tiptoed to where he kept the golden box and quietly tipped back the lid.

Immediately, a cyclone of ills came rushing out—sorrows and disease, famine and disaster, greed and pollution, poverty and pain. Pandora slammed the lid as fast as she could, but every evil had escaped. Plagues swirled around her in a foul-smelling spiral, growing wider and wider until they spread to every corner of Earth. Prometheus's chunk of coal, however, lay trapped inside the golden box.

Now a great wailing of grief and anguish rose from humankind. On the highest peak of Mount Caucasus, Prometheus heard the chaos. *The plagues of Zeus!* he realized. *He's sent his box to Earth and unleashed its evils!*

Pandora went to her grave with her secret sin untold. For a thousand years the human race suffered the punishments of Zeus. And for just as long, Prometheus froze and burned in his chains and bore his agonizing exile.

Epimetheus watched generations of humans suffer plagues and disasters. He saw greed and jealousy and lust destroy lives. He was unable to help. Although forbidden, he returned to the mountaintop and his captive brother. "I do not understand," cried Epimetheus. "The humans are dying, suffering as you suffer."

"Zeus has tricked you," Prometheus said. "Tell me,

did he ever give you a golden box?"

"Many, many years ago. It was a wedding gift to my wife. I had forgotten all about it."

"Find it! Find it and take it to the strongest mortal you know."

"Why, that would be Hercules," Epimetheus said. "He has succeeded at every labor ever assigned to him by the gods."

"Tell Hercules to open the box. Tell him to light a fire on Earth with the tiny chunk of coal he finds inside. Then he must swallow the chunk. It will fill him with the thing he needs to free me!"

Epimetheus and Hercules carried out their instructions. Hephaestus had been watching from Mount Olympus, and now he descended to Earth to make right a wrong he had done many, many years ago. He melted the golden box into a gleaming arrowhead and gave it to Hercules. The strongest of all mortals gazed at the distant peak of Caucasus. He knew what he must do.

All that day and all through the night, Hercules climbed. Loose rocks kicked out beneath him. He slipped and plunged, but dug in again and struggled upward. At dawn, he reached Prometheus. It was feeding time for the vulture of Zeus. "Slay the evil beast!" Prometheus begged.

As the buzzard dove to rip Prometheus's flesh, Hercules let his arrow fly. The golden tip pierced the vulture's leathery throat and broke its neck. A howl thundered from Mount Olympus. "NO!" Zeus hurled a thunderbolt, but the mortal caught it in his powerful fist.

"Stretch your chains," he told Prometheus. Then he

smashed the lightning bolt down upon the links, breaking them one by one. With each strike, Zeus felt the sinews of his power snap.

The sun swelled over the horizon. Prometheus stood unbound at last atop the mountain—free! For the first time in one thousand years, he greeted the sunrise with arms outspread in joy.

On Mount Olympus, Zeus was sulking. Prometheus approached him, followed by Epimetheus and Hercules. "I have a proposal," Prometheus said. "The mortals have agreed to offer you more than bones in sacrifice, if you will agree to rule side by side with my wisdom and love."

Centuries of weariness had weakened Zeus's resolve. "I agree," he muttered.

Now Epimetheus stepped forward. "One question burns in my heart, brother. What was in the coal that you placed inside the golden box?"

Zeus glanced up.

"Hope," said Prometheus. "Look below and you will see flames ignited by the tiniest spark of hope."

Epimetheus and Hercules, and Zeus as well, turned and saw the fires that would never, never die.